חובות הלבבות
שער חשבון הנפש ואהבת השם

DUTIES OF THE HEART
*The Gates of Introspection
and Love of God*

RABBEINU BACHYA IBN PAKUDA

Translated and Annotated by
Avraham Yaakov Finkel

YESHIVATH BETH MOSHE
SCRANTON, PA.

CONTENTS

הקדמה
מראש הישיבה
מורינו הרב יעקב שניידמאן שליט"א

יוצר העולם ובורא הכל ברא את העולם בחשבון מדויק וכן כל בריאה ובריאה בפרטו מתקיים רק בחשבון. אלו היה כדור הארץ קרוב יותר מעט לשמש היה חום השמש שורף הכל ואילו היה רחוק מעט יותר היה הקור מתגבר ולא היו הבריות מתקיימים. יש נברא־ים שהאור מזיק להם ויש שצריכים אור ואפילו הם תוספת האור מזיק להם. יש נבראים שצריכים לחות ויש שצריכים יבישות. יש אילנות שגדלים מגשם הרבה ויש שהרבה גשם מזיק להם.

וכן האדם בריאתו הוא בדיוק נפלא וחשבון עמוק. כל אבר שבגופו מתאים עם שאר האברים וכולם פועלים פעולתם בדקדוק. הלב דופק במנין מדויק אילו היה דופק במהירות או במתינות ממה שהוא צריך לא היה האדם יכול לחיות חיים נורמלים. אילו האדם היה משתין יותר מדי היה מזיק לו הרבה וכו'. והמעיין קצת יראה בכל דבר ממש חשבון ע"פ חשבון.

וכמו שנברא העולם בחשבון כן מעשי האדם לפרנס עצמו הוא בחשבון, ובלא חשבון יאבד הכל. כשהאיכר זורע שדהו אינו זורע אלא בזמן הראוי ובמקום הראוי. כשבונה ביתו עושה חשבון על כל פרט ופרט מהבנין, וכן תקיש לכל מעשיהו.

ואם כל זה בעניינים גשמיים על אחת כמה וכמה בעניינים רוחני־ים החשבון מדוייק אפילו יותר. ולכן סידר הקב"ה את התורה בחשב־ון מדוייק עבור נפש האדם. עונשי התורה אינם עונשים מקריים על שלא נזהר בציווי מלכו של עולם אלא הם תוצאות העבירה ממש וכמו שאמרו שכר עבירה עבירה וכמו שימות מי שאוכל סם המות

כן ממש הוא עונש העבירה. וכל עבירה מכוון בחשבון מדוייק בהזיקו ופעלו. וכן הוא במצות שכל מצוה הוא לצורך האדם להעמידו על קו היושר שלא יטבע בים החומריות, ושבת ויום טוב נתנו להשפיע שפע מיוחד של קדושה בכל זמן כפי מה שהוא צריך. ומה שכתבנו אינו אפילו כפתחו של מחט בהבנת עומק יסוד המצות ושכרן.

הרי נתברר שאם יעמוד האדם רק כרגע להתבונן על מהלך העולם בכללו ועל מצות התורה ישתומם מעומק ודקדוק החשבון שבהם. ולפי"ז היה נראה אך למותר לעורר לאדם לעשות חשבון בנפשו בכל מה שעושה ולהתבונן אם מקיים חיובו כראוי אך לדאבוננו לא כן הוא אלא רוב בני אדם הולכים במרוצת הרגלם ורצים דחופים להשיג מה שאין בכחם להשיג ואינם משימין לב על דרכיהם לעשות חשבון הראוי וכבר נתעורר על זה המסילת ישרים בפרק ב' וז"ל דזה מתחבולות היצה"ר וערמתו להכביד עבודתו בתמידות על לבות בני אדם, עד שלא ישאר להם כח להתבונן ולהסתכל באיזה דרך הם הולכים. כי יודע הוא שאילולי היו שמים לבם כמעט קט על דרכיהם, ודאי שמיד היו מתחילים לנחם ממעשיהם עכ"ל. והוא מפלאי הבריאה ומדין הבחירה שהאדם אף שכל סביבותיו הכל הולך בחשבון מדוייק מ"מ ניסת הוא ע"י היצה"ר שלא לעשות חשבון לנפשו.

והנה מה שבעל חובות הלבבות סידר שער חשבון הנפש קרוב לסוף הספר לא מפני קלות חיובו ולומר שרק לאחר קניית כל המעלות עוד נוסף עליו חיוב לעשות חשבון לנפשו דבודאי חשבון הנפש הוא התחלת הכל אלא שהוצרך להקדים אליו שאר השערים כדי שיקנה הכלים והידיעות לעשות חשבון הגון, וסוף דבר במחשבה תחילה וכל הספר כהקדמה לשער הזה.

יוצר הכל ובעל החשבון האמיתי ישפיע לן השכל והרצון לעשות חשבון הנפש כראוי ועי"ז נזכה ליהנות מזיו השכינה.

TRANSLATION OF RABBI YAAKOV
SCHNAIDMAN'S PROLOGUE

Hashem, in creating the world, did so with precise calculations. The earth's orbit around the sun is close enough for the sun's warmth to sustain life, but yet not so close that it will be burnt from the sun's heat. Some forms of life are disturbed by light, while others need light to survive. Certain creatures need an abundance of moisture, and some thrive in a basically dry environment. Some trees grow only in a rain forest while others cannot put up with so much rain.

So too, man was created with extraordinary precision. All of his limbs work in conjunction with each other to accomplish their precise task. The heart pumps in an exact cycle, if it would slow down or go faster than its required speed, the person could not lead a normal life. The same is true for all his bodily functions. With just a small amount of effort, the precise calculations all around him become obvious.

Just as the world was created with great precision, so too, man, to acquire his livelihood, must work with great precision. The farmer must plant at just the right moment and in the proper place. The builder must make many intricate calculations for every detail. This follows for all types of work.

If this is so for things in the physical realm, surely this must be so when it comes to the spiritual realm. Hashem gave us the Torah, calculating perfectly what is beneficial for the soul of man. The

punishment for transgressing the Torah is not meted out simply because the person disobeyed, but rather, the transgression itself
brings him punishment, just as one will die when he eats poison.
There is an exact calculation of the destruction brought by each
transgression. The same is true when one fulfills the mitzvos. Each
mitzvah is necessary to raise man spiritually so that he does not sink
into physicality. For example, Shabbos and Yom Tov are times to
acquire special holiness that is manifest on those days.

It is clear that if one would only stop and contemplate the wonders of this world and the mitzvos of the Torah, he would be overwhelmed by the depth and the precision of its design. This being
so, it would seem superfluous to point out that one must make precise calculations and be introspective to ensure that he is fulfilling
his duty at all times. But, alas, most people follow the path they are
used to, and get so involved in their activities that they don't pay
attention to their actions and accomplishments and don't make a
proper accounting for their deeds. The Mesillas Yesharim writes
"This is the trap of the *yetzer hara* and his trickery, he causes people to toil excessively and constantly, until they don't have the
strength to be introspective, to see which path they are following,
because he knows, that if they would only stop and pay attention
to what they are doing, they would immediately begin to regret
their actions." This is truly one of the unfathomable designs of creation, that, although naturally one should be compelled by the precision of the world around him to make an accounting for himself,
still, to allow for free will, Hashem gave the *yetzer hara* the power
to make one oblivious to the world in which he lives.

The author of Duties of the Heart placed the Gate of Introspection towards the end of the book. This was not because it is unim-
portant, but, rather because before having acquired the other qualities it would be impossible to make a proper accounting. The pre-
ceding Gates are like an introduction to this Gate.

The Creator and true calculator should grant us the intelligence
and will, to be introspective and make proper calculations, and
thereby meriting to bask in His Glorious Splendor.

DUTIES OF THE HEART
GATE EIGHT

———◉———

The Gate of Introspection
Examining One's Inner Self
Before God

INTRODUCTION

———◆———

T he previous gate dealt with the elements of repentance, one of which is introspection. It is fitting to follow with an explanation of introspection, since it stimulates one to act in ways that will benefit him in both worlds, as David said, *"I have considered my ways, and have returned to Your decrees"* (*Tehillim* 119:59).

I will expound on six areas:

ONE: The definition of introspection.

TWO: Must everyone be introspective in the same way?

THREE: The many ways a person should examine his inner self.

FOUR: The benefits of introspection.

FIVE: Must one examine his inner self all the time?

SIX: The course of action to take after introspection.

CHAPTER ONE

THE DEFINITION OF INTROSPECTION

———=◉=———

Introspection is the soul-searching one does concerning his Torah observance and his conduct in worldly matters, in order to ascertain what he has already accomplished, and what he has yet to accomplish.

Moshe Rabbeinu instructed us to do so when he said, *"Realize it today and ponder it in your heart, that God is the Supreme Being"* (*Devarim* 4:39), and David said, *"Taste and see how good God is"* (*Tehillim* 34:9), *"Know the God of your father and serve Him"* (1 *Divrei Hayamim* 28:9), and *"Do not be like a senseless horse or mule"* (*Tehillim* 32:9). About those who do not reflect about their spiritual condition nor analyze their inner selves it says, *"They do not give thought, they lack knowledge and judgment"* (*Yeshayah* 44:19), and, *"They did not remember His strength"* (*Tehillim* 78:42). [About one who contemplates the kindness we received from God, it says] *"Recall the days of old"* (*Devarim* 32:7), and, *"I will come to insight from afar"* (*Iyov* 36:3).

CHAPTER TWO

MUST EVERYONE BE INTROSPECTIVE IN THE SAME WAY?

People have different aspirations about Torah observance and worldly obligations depending on their intelligence and ability to grasp ideas. According to one's ability to recognize God's goodness toward the Jewish people in general and to himself in particular, one must search his heart to determine whether he has done all he is obligated to do, in serving the Creator.

Moshe Rabbeinu said, *"You must now realize that I am not speaking of your children, who did not know and did not see the lesson that God your Lord taught. . . But your own eyes have seen all the great deeds God has done" (Devarim 11:2,7)*. Moshe explained to the Jewish people involved in the exodus from Egypt, that the Creator's demands on them are much stronger than any demands on their children. The children did not witness the Creator's miracles like the Generation of the Exodus. Those, who saw the miracles with their own eyes, who experienced great favors, who were rescued from the plagues that were brought on Egypt and on Korach and his party, have a greater obligation to serve God out of gratitude. The same is true today. Not everyone has the same obligation to serve God. It depends on his intelligence and on the favors he received from God. [The more perceptive he is and the more favors he received, the more intensely he must serve God.] A believer should reflect on his obligations to God, and meticulously carry them out to the best of his understanding. Those mitzvos that he can do himself, he should perform as painstakingly as he can; those that cannot be done personally he should fulfill by studying about them and yearning to do them, as David said, [about the Torah and the mitzvos], *"I only wish that my ways were firm in keeping Your laws" (Tehillim 119:5),* and, *"More desirable than much gold, and fine gold, sweeter than honey and the drippings of the comb [are the Torah and the mitzvos]" (ibid. 19:11).*

If you do this, the Creator will judge you favorably [and take into account that you did not perform these mitzvos because you were unable to do so]. But this is only if you set your heart on fulfilling these obligations to your Creator when the opportunity arises. For if when the opportunity arises, you look for excuses to get around doing your duty, and belittle, neglect or ignore it, you will be sorry on the great Day of Reckoning, as it says, *"He who disdains a precept will be injured thereby" (Mishlei 13:13).*

CHAPTER THREE

THE MANY WAYS A PERSON SHOULD EXAMINE HIS INNER SELF

———◈———

There are many ways to analyze how well you are doing your duty toward God. I will present thirty of them, which if you take to heart, will help you understand your duties to God.

GOD TAKES CARE OF YOU

ONE: Reflect on your origins—how you came into existence from non-existence and were transformed from nothingness to life, not because you deserved it, but because of God's kindness, goodness and generosity. You will realize how much more important, exalted, and noble you are than animals, plants and minerals, and you will recognize how grateful you should be to the Creator.

To draw an analogy, imagine that as an infant your mother abandoned you in the street and a passing stranger saw you, took pity on you, took you home, cared for you and raised you until you were a grown and mature man. Imagine how obligated you would be to this person. Imagine how much you would owe this person in every way. Then consider how God cares for you and provides all your needs. Surely you should feel compelled to serve Him and do His mitzvos.

Moshe Rabbeinu admonished the Jewish people about this, saying, *"Is this the way you repay Your God, you ungrateful, unwise nation? Is He not your Father, your Master, the One who made and established you?" (Devarim 32:6)*, and Yechezkel elaborated on this theme in the chapter that contains the verse, *"On the day you were born you were left dying, rejected in an open field. When I passed by you and saw you wallowing in your blood, I said to you, 'In your blood you shall live, in your blood you shall live!'" (Yechezkel 16:6)*.

GOD FASHIONED YOU PERFECTLY

TWO: Consider how generous God has been to you; how perfectly he has structured your body, outlined your shape, refined your mental powers, and modeled your limbs. In his kindness, He helped you leave your mother's womb, and provided you with just the right amount of nourishment before and after birth. Imagine that you were born without eyes, hands or feet; now imagine how grateful and appreciative you would be to a person who provided you with these, making you complete. How eagerly you would do his bidding and how avidly you would serve him! That is how eager you should be to do the Creator's bidding, and how avidly you should serve Him, for He formed your body and shaped your limbs to absolute perfection. Iyov had this in mind when he said, *"Consider that You fashioned me like clay, will You then turn me back into dust? You poured me out like milk, congealed me like cheese. You clothed me with skin and flesh and wove me of bones and sinews" (Iyov 10:9)*, and it says, *"It was You Who created my organs" (Tehillim 139:13); "You drew me from the womb, made me secure at my mother's breast" (ibid. 22:10)*.

GOD GAVE YOU YOUR INTELLECT

THREE: Contemplate how good God has been to you by granting you a thinking, perceptive mind and many noble qualities that make you superior to unintelligent animals. As it says, *"Who gives us more knowledge than the beasts of the earth, makes us wiser than the birds of the sky?" (Iyov 35:11).*

Picture yourself a mindless boor. If someone helped you to become intelligent, you would certainly recognize how much better off you are. Would a lifetime be enough to thank that person and repay him? How much more are you indebted to the Creator, Whose favors and kindnesses are endless, as it says, *"You, O God my Lord, have done many things; the wonders You have devised for us— none can compare to You" (Tehillim 40:6).*

GOD GAVE YOU THE TORAH

FOUR: Be mindful of God's greatest gift—that he made you aware of the magnificent Torah which sustains your life in this world and in the World to Come. It does away with your [spiritual] blindness, lights up your eyes, draws you closer to God's will, and makes known to you the true [perspective] on the Creator and your obligations to Him, in order to enable you to attain perfect happiness in both worlds. As it says, *"God's Torah is perfect, it restores the soul. God's testimony is trustworthy, it makes the simple one wise. God's orders are upright, they gladden the heart" (Tehillim 19:8,9).*

Imagine, that you knew the inestimable value of the Torah, yet it was beyond your understanding. Someone helped you [understand it and taught you how to perform the mitzvos]. Would all your efforts to thank him be equal to the favor he has done you? How much more so are you unable to thank the Creator, Who encourages you through the Torah to do your duties, and Who helps you understand it and observe it. The least you can do to express your gratitude is to dedicate yourself fervently to His Torah and eagerly take upon yourself to keep his mitzvos. For it says, *"I have hurried and not delayed to keep Your mitzvos" (Tehillim 119:60); "O how I love Your Torah, it is my study all day long" (ibid. 119:97); "How pleasing is Your word to My palate" (ibid. 119:103).*

APPLY YOURSELF TO STUDY THE TORAH

FIVE: Realize how lax you are in understanding God's Torah and how complacent you are about your shallow Torah knowledge. You would not act this way if you were unsure of the meaning of a book you received from a king. If you were bewildered, by the handwriting, the meaning of a phrase, the fine points of a knotty concept, or by its convoluted style of writing, you would make every effort to understand it.

If you go to such lengths to grasp the work of a mere mortal, shouldn't you apply yourself even more diligently to understand God's Book which is your life, as it says, *"It is your life and the length of your days" (Devarim 30:20)?*

How can you allow yourself to neglect the Torah, by being content with only a superficial understanding of parts of it and passing by the rest. You are behaving like the person about whom it says, *"You have praised the gods of silver and gold, bronze and iron, wood and stone, which do not see, hear or understand; but the God Who controls your lifebreath and every move you make—Him you did not glorify" (Daniel 5:23).*

DISOBEDIENCE BRINGS RUIN IN ITS WAKE

SIX: Search your heart when you sense in yourself a tendency to rebel against the Creator and the covenant He made with you [to keep His mitzvos]. Reflect, that everything you observe in the sky above and on earth below, is God's creation and follows God's laws [of nature]. Has one of these elements ever resigned from the task God set for it, rebelled against His word, or backed out of His covenant?

If one of the elements reneged on God's covenant by changing its nature, mankind would cease to exist. Were the earth to leave its position at the center of the universe, or the ocean to overflow its boundaries and flood the earth, would there be a single person left on earth?

Consider your limbs. Were they to break the Creator's covenant—movable limbs becoming rigid, and rigid ones becoming movable—or your senses would stop operating, all your bodily functions would cease. How can you be unashamed to violate God's covenant in the world that has not, and how can you transgress using the organs that are dutybound to serve God and carry out His directives?

Let me offer the following analogy: A king commanded a group of his servants to care for one of his ministers. He was to be taken across a [raging] river to a place where he would stay for some time. The king told the minister to do certain things for the servants in return. The servants carried out the king's order, but the minister did not.

One of the servants said to the minister, "Your excellency! You are ignoring the king's order! Aren't you afraid that we too, might ignore the king's order to guard you? Why don't you repent, because the king has ordered us to stop keeping an eye on you if you ignore his order regarding us." The minister realized his mistake and corrected his oversight.

Dear brother, consider this: Have your limbs ever failed to comply with God's command when you used them? The Creator stipulated in His faithful Torah that everything in the world is yours to do with as you wish, as long as you serve Him, but that everything in the world will work against you if you defy His word.

BE A FAITHFUL SERVANT OF GOD

SEVEN: Analyze whether you relate to God like a servant to his master, fulfilling the duties a master demands of his servant. This subject was discussed at length in the fourth chapter of the Gate of Service to the Creator.

Think about your obligations to God. Bear in mind that the Creator constantly does favors for you, provides for your needs, is merciful to you, and supplies you with all the food you need. He did not leave you to fend for yourself with a feeble intellect, rather, He gave you wisdom, insight and understanding to guide you in your worldly needs and enable you to understand your duties to Him, as David said, *"I am Your servant—give me understanding"* (*Tehillim 119:125*).

When you—the servant—recognize the signs of your Master's extraordinary kindness to your soul, your body and motions, and the fact that He observes you always and knows your overt and concealed qualities as He watches your movements, controlling and directing them; when you realize that He tests you by giving you freedom to use your limbs and to be swayed by either your *yetzer hatov* or your *yetzer hara*; and when you realize that God gave us the Torah letting us know what pleases or angers Him—then you will use your limbs and your mental faculties to please God, and draw closer to Him. You will cast off the veil of the evil impulse [that prevents you from recognizing the countless kindnesses God bestows on you], becoming awestruck and humble before Him, loving Him, and wanting only what He wants.

When you do this, generous bounty awaits you and great illumination will be showered on you, as it says, *"They walk in the light of Your Presence"* (*Tehillim 89:16*), and, *"May God make His Presence enlighten you and grant you grace"* (*Numbers 6:25*).

The most important thing a servant can do is wholeheartedly accept God alone as his Master. His love for Him will then be complete, and he will be loved in return. As it says, *"Today you have declared allegiance to God . . . God has similarly declared allegiance to you today, making you His special nation . . . He will make you the highest of all nations"* (*Devarim 26:17-19*), and, *"All the nations of the world will realize that God's name is associated with you, and they will be in awe of you"* (*ibid. 28:10*).

The nations will be in awe of the Jewish people because a servant's prestige corresponds to his master's prestige, and rises to the degree the master favors him. Since the Creator's name is elevated and exalted in the eyes of the nations, as it says, *"For from where the sun rises to where it sets, My name is honored among the nations"* (*Malachi 1:11*), and since the nation closest to Him and chosen to serve Him is the Jewish people, it follows that our prestige is higher than that of the other nations.

The meaning of the above-mentioned passage, *God's name is associated with you* is that He has called us *People of God, the Lord's People, Priests of God, Servants of God, Children of God* and similar names denoting preference from among other nations. The meaning of the phrase, *[the nations] will be in awe of you* is that the nations will treat us with respect out of reverence for the Creator, as it says, *"Who would not revere You, O King of the nations?"* (*Yirmeyah 10:7*).

The following passage expresses the closeness to God and total commitment to His service that we will attain in time to come. *"One person will say, 'I belong to God,' another will use the name of 'Jacob,' another will mark his arm, 'Belongs to God,' and adopt the name of 'Israel.'"* (*Isaiah 44:5*). The different phrases people will adopt reflect their degree of closeness to God, and how fervently they serve Him.

Reflect on this and don't be misled by your *yetzer hara* nor be swayed by your physical desires. The Creator observes your self-analysis, so do it for His sake, in a spirit of humility, for God reads your thoughts, as it says, *"God knows the thoughts of man to be futile"* (*Tehillim 94:11*).

BEING WHOLEHEARTEDLY DEVOTED TO GOD

EIGHT: Question whether you are wholeheartedly devoted to God. One must be wholeheartedly devoted to God in two ways. Firstly by accepting His Oneness, as we explained at the beginning of this book; and secondly by being devoted to Him alone when you are doing any action that has to do with the World to Come— whether obligatory or optional—as we explained in the fifth Gate of this book.

The way to accept God's Oneness is to have no other god, and not to attribute to Him form, shape, likeness, quality, movement, change, physicality, or anything having to do with essence or char-acteristic. Accepting God's Oneness consists of believing that He has no beginning and no end; that He is One, and that there is no oneness like His; and that there is no other creator or maker, and nothing to share His great Name and glorious attributes.

The way to devote your actions to God is to do them exclusive-ly for the sake of His great Name. Don't do them for love of praise by others, in hopes of reward, for fear of others, to gain an advan-tage, or to avoid loss in this world or the next. As our Sages put it, "Do not be like servants who serve their master for the sake of re-ceiving a reward; instead, be like servants who serve their master not for the sake of receiving a reward" (Avos 1:3).

Watch how friends act; when one realizes that the other is not sincere in his friendship he becomes angry, and nothing the friend does pleases him, even if he outwardly seems to be sincere. [He is angry] despite the fact that he needs his friend and depends on his help. All the more so, must we be devoted wholeheartedly to the Creator, Whom everyone needs, Who needs no one, and Who ben-efits from no one, Who reads our thoughts and knows our inner-most secrets. How can we please God by acting in ways we would not dare act toward our friends and neighbors who cannot see the deceit buried in our hearts?

A person understanding this will turn pale with shame before the Creator. He will put his inner self in order and devote himself to God, sincerely believing in God's Oneness, doing the mitzvos and learning Torah purely for the sake of God, as David said, *"I will run in the way of Your commandments"* (Tehillim 119:32).

SERVING GOD WITH PROPER CONCENTRATION

NINE: Determine whether you are serving God with the same ded-ication you would serve a king.

If a king ordered you to do something involving physical labor, you would spare no effort to carry it out. If the king's order required study, thought and counsel, you would focus your thoughts, intellect, brainpower and discernment to bring the project at hand to completion. If you wanted to praise and thank the king for his kindness in poem or in prose, in writing or verbally, you would create the most polished verses you can think of. You would praise the king with exaggerated titles, overstating his accomplishments without regard to the true facts. In fact, if you could demonstrate your feeling through your limbs to sing his praises, you would. If you could move heaven and earth and everything in them to join you in a mighty chorus of gratitude, you would do that, too. And you would do all this for a king who is a frail and insignificant human being, whose days pass very quickly. An intelligent person should surely do the same when serving God.

All things you do for the sake of God fall into one of three categories: they are either one of the duties of the heart [such as believing in God, loving Him, loving your neighbor, not being envious, not bearing a grudge, not taking revenge]; or a combination of the duties of the heart and physical duties, like prayer, Torah study, praising and glorifying God, studying science [which is helpful toward understanding the Torah], encouraging others to do good and to stay away from evil, and the like; or physical mitzvos that do not involve the heart, other than that at the outset you must have the intention of doing the mitzvah for the sake of God, like *sukkah, lulav, tzitzis, mezuzah, Shabbos, Yamim Tovim*, giving charity, and other such mitzvos. These physical mitzvos are not invalidated when you are distracted while doing them, but when you are engaged in duties of the heart you have to clear your mind of all worldly thoughts, devoting your full attention and inner being to God alone.

In fact, they say that one of the holy men used to add the following to his prayers: "My God, the anguish I feel because I do not serve You as I should has supplanted all other pain, and the anxiety I feel because I am so distant from You has supplanted all other anxieties." If you have this attitude [and clear your mind of all distractions], God will accept your service and will be pleased with you. Concerning these mitzvos, our Sages said: "Mitzvos must be done with the proper intention" (Rosh Hashanah 28b).

A Discourse on Prayer

When doing a mitzvah that combines duties of the heart and a physical duty, such as praying and singing God's praises, cleanse your body by washing away any filth and stand far from anything foul-smelling. Then stop all mundane and other religious activities and clear all distracting thoughts from your mind. Next, concentrate on to Whom you are directing your prayers, what you are asking from Him, and the meaning of the words of your prayer.

The words of prayer you utter with your tongue are like the peel of a fruit, whereas reflecting on the meaning of the words is the fruit itself. Prayers are the body, and concentrating on them is the soul. When you pray with your tongue but your thoughts are preoccupied with other things, your prayer is a body without a soul, a peel without the fruit—your body is there, but your mind is elsewhere. God said in Scripture about such a person, *"Because the people have approached [Me] with their mouths and honored Me with their lips, while they kept their heart far from Me. . ." (Isaiah 29:13).*

[If you pray without concentrating on the meaning of your prayer,] you are like the servant whose master was a guest in his house. The servant told his wife and children to honor the master and wait on him. But, instead of personally serving his master and attending to his needs, the servant went away. The master became angry with the servant and did not accept the honor and service provided by the family. So too, if you pray without your thoughts and soul taking part, God will reject the prayer because it is only the empty action of your body and tongue.

We end the *Shemoneh esrei* with the words, *"May the words of my mouth and the musings of my heart be acceptable to You" (Tehillim 19:15).* If you think of worldly matters while praying—no matter whether the subject is permitted or forbidden—and then conclude your prayer with the words, *May the musings of my heart be acceptable to You,* you are guilty of a shocking offense. You claim to have spoken to God with your heart and soul, but you did not, and then you ask Him to accept your prayer and be pleased with it. You are like the people about whom it says, *"They [pretend to] seek Me daily, eager to learn My ways, as if they were a nation that does what is right, [but in reality they pay only lip service]"* *(Yeshayah 58:2).*

Our Sages said: "Always take stock of yourself: If you can concentrate while praying, pray, if not, do not pray" (Berachos 28b). We are also told that one of the things Rabbi Eliezer, said to his students on his death bed was, "When you pray, know before Whom you are standing" (Berachos 28b). Furthermore it says, *"Prepare to meet your God, O Israel"* *(Amos 4:12),* Our Sages said: "Do not make your prayer a set routine, rather beg for compassion and mercy from the Almighty" (Avos 2:13), as it says, *"When my soul was immersed in prayer, I remembered God"* *(Jonah 2:8),* and *"Let us lift our hearts and hands to God in Heaven"* *(Eichah 3:41).*

The idea of prayer is to express the soul's yearning for God and its submission to Him; to exalt, to praise, and thank His Name, and to cast all one's burdens upon Him.

Since it is hard to remember all these ideas, our Sages formulated [a set text for prayer] and included the basic needs of most people, which demonstrate our dependence on God and our submission to Him. These are the basic prayers arranged in proper order. With them, you can approach the Creator without being ashamed [of asking for something unwarranted, or being unable to express your thoughts], and you verbalize words of submission and humility.

Our sages formulated a set text, not leaving the text up to the individual, because our thoughts are erratic, passing quickly through our mind and making it difficult to concentrate on our prayers. When you verbalize prayers in an orderly fashion, and enunciate a prepared text it is easier to concentrate on the words.

Prayer is comprised of spoken words and thoughts. While the words need thought [to make them meaningful], thought does not need spoken words [to give it meaning]; it is possible to perceive an idea in your mind [without verbalizing it]. The thought—the meaning of prayer—is the essential part and purpose of prayer. This is borne out by our Sages who said, "A ritually unclean person should say the words of the *Shema* mentally without saying a *berachah* before and after" (Berachos 20b). Furthermore, they said that [in an emergency] you are allowed to say an abbreviated *Shemoneh esrei*, [now if the words were the essence of prayer, we would not be permitted to skip any of them under any circumstances.]

Arrange your prayers in your mind, so that your thoughts will be in harmony with the words you say, with both your words and thoughts focused on God alone. While praying, keep your body motionless, and don't consider any worldly things. Act as if you were in the presence of a [mortal] king whom you were thanking and praising, and whose kindness you were describing, though a king does not know your innermost thoughts and cannot be compared to the Creator Who observes your outward and inward life, your hidden and your revealed sides.

God trusted you to pray properly and no one but God knows what is in your heart when you are praying. If you pray as God has commanded you to, you are worthy of the trust that He placed in you, and He will accept your prayers. As David said, about those worthy of this trust *"My eyes are on the faithful men of the land, to have them at my side, he who follows the way of the blameless shall be in my service" (Tehillim 101:6)*. If you do not pray with your heart and your tongue as you should, you have betrayed the trust that has been placed in you, and you are among those that are described in the verse, *"They are a generation that reverses itself and cannot be trusted" (Devarim 32:20)*.

When you fulfill a physical mitzvah, like *sukkah, lulav*, or the like, begin by directing your thoughts to God. That way your deed will be rooted in obedience to God's mitzvos, and thereby you will magnify, exalt, thank and praise Him for His great favors and His abundant kindness. You will do the mitzvah to perfection from beginning to end with fear of God and with a desire to do His will and to avoid His anger, as David said, *"To do what pleases You, my God, is my desire" (Tehillim 40:9)*.

When doing a mitzvah, keep in mind how you would act if a king asked you to do something. You will then find energy and eagerness in your limbs to serve God, as David said, *"I have considered my ways, and have turned back to Your decrees. I have hurried and not delayed to keep Your commandments" (Tehillim 119:59,60)*.

GOD SEES EVERYTHING YOU DO AND THINK

TEN: The Creator sees your outer and inner self. He watches and remembers all your actions and thoughts, both the good and the bad. Always be in awe of Him, and try to improve your outer and inner life to live up to His will.

If your boss, or a person who had done you a favor was observing every move you made, would you do something to offend him? Certainly not. Surely if the One Who observes you is the Creator, you should be abashed in His Presence, careful not to rebel against Him, and eager to serve Him and win His favor and love.

We dress in our best clothing when we meet a king, a president, or a prominent personality, because they pay attention to how we look. As it says, *"It is forbidden to enter the king's gate wearing sackcloth"* (Esther 4:2), and, *"Pharaoh sent messengers and had Joseph summoned. They rushed him from the dungeon. He cut his hair and changed his clothes, and then came to Pharaoh"* (Bereishis 41:14). Similarly, we should adorn ourselves before God outwardly and inwardly when we serve Him, because He watches us all the time. If a king were to observe your inner self the way he noticed your outward appearance, you would surely enhance your inner self to please him.

People learn and teach different fields of study only to impress the people in power, and people obey the law simply because they are ordered to do so by the government. That being so, we should surely enhance ourselves before God in our conscience, our hearts, and our limbs [i.e. our actions], because He constantly watches over them, and nothing distracts Him, as it says, *"I God, probe the heart, search the mind . . .(Yirmeyah 17:10)*; *"The eyes of God are everywhere, observing the bad and the good"* (Mishlei 15:3); *"The eyes of God, they scan the whole world"* (Zechariah 4:10). Be in awe of God because He watches you, as it says, *"Be not rash with your mouth, and let not your heart be hasty to utter a word before God; for God is in heaven and you are on earth"* (Koheles 5:1), and, *"God looks down from heaven on mankind"* (Tehillim 14:2).

If you are mindful of this, the Creator will be with you, and you will sense His Presence. You will be in awe of Him, exalt Him, reflect on His works, and ponder the way He guides the world that bears witness to His greatness, magnificence, wisdom and power.

Do this continuously and God will remove your sadness and your fear [of stumbling into sin]. He will open the gates of knowledge of Him for you, and reveal the secrets of His wisdom to you. He will guide and care for you, rather than leave you to your own devices, as it says, *"God is my shepherd, I lack nothing"* (Tehillim 23:1).

You will attain the loftiest level of piety, a stage attained only by the righteous. You will see without eyes, hear without ears, speak without a tongue, feel without senses, and understand things [intuitively].

Nothing will make you unhappy, and you will not like anything better than what God has provided for you. You will love what God loves and despise what He despises. The wise Shlomoh described such a person, saying, *"Happy is the man who listens to Me, coming early to My gates each day, waiting outside My doors. For he who finds Me finds life and obtains favor from God"* (Mishlei 8:34,35).

TAKE STOCK OF YOUR SERVICE TO GOD

ELEVEN: Have you engaged in the service of God, or catered to your *yetzer hara?*

Imagine that a king gave you money for a project, and warned you against using it for another purpose. He explained that he would demand an accounting of your expenditures at the end of the year, not forgiving the smallest discrepancy. You would audit your account every month scrupulously watching every penny. The final accounting would not find you unprepared, of knowing your credits and debits.

Likewise, take stock every day as to whether you served God as you should. If you were lax about this accounting until now, begin today. Don't [think it is too late to begin], because this will pile new negligence on top of past negligence and new evasion on top of old evasion. Remember God does not neglect, evade or forget.

Days are like scrolls; record on each "scroll" that for which you would like to be remembered. As it says, *"Be not like a senseless horse or mule" (Tehillim 32:9)*, and it says about a person who puts off taking stock of himself, *"Gray hairs have sprouted, and still he has taken no notice" (Hoshea 7:9)*.

PURSUE SPIRITUAL RATHER THAN MATERIAL VALUES

TWELVE: See how zealous you are about worldly matters, devoting your talents to them, and how disdainful you are about your after-life, straying from the right path of serving God.

Your worldly thoughts are uppermost in your mind, your worldly aspirations are your primary concern, and your possessions do not satisfy you; the more you have, the more you want. Like fire, the more fuel you add, the bigger the flame. Day and night, your thoughts are focused on worldly things to such an extent that you count as a friend only he who can further your ambitions, as a trusted companion only he who can make your dreams come true. You anxiously anticipate opportunities to buy or sell merchandise, and you follow the shifting market conditions and price fluctuations all over the world. Nothing discourages you from traveling to distant places. Neither heat nor cold, stormy seas nor lengthy desert passages deter you [from making a profit]. You do not consider the possibility that your hard work may be in vain, and that all you will have to show for your exertion is pain and drudgery. And even if you earn the profit you were hoping to realize, you may only have it to manage and keep until the rightful owner gets it, [which will happen] either in your lifetime, as it says, *"In the middle of his life [his wealth] will leave him" (Yirmeyah 17:11)*, or sometime after your passing, as it says, *"They leave their wealth to others" (Tehillim 49:11)*.

The wise Shlomoh warned us not be zealous in amassing wealth, saying, *"Do not toil to gain wealth, have the sense to desist"* *(Mishlei 23:4).* He described the disease associated with it, saying, *"You see it, then it is gone; it grows wings and flies away"* *(ibid. v. 5).* King David taught us to earn only what we need, saying, *"When you enjoy the fruit of your labors, you are praiseworthy, and it is well with you"* *(Tehillim 128:2).* In this vein, the pious man [Agur ben Yakeh] asked God to grant him enough income to sustain him, but to prevent him from becoming either wealthy—because it would turn him into a pleasure seeker; or poor—because it would undermine his ethics and his Torah learning. He said, *"I ask two things of You . . . give me neither poverty nor wealth, but allot me my daily bread, lest I be sated and deny You . . . . and lest I become impoverished and steal and take the Name of my God [in a vain oath of innocence]"* *(Mishlei 30:7).* Similarly, we find Yaakov our father asked God to give him only his bare necessities, saying, *"Give me food to eat and clothing to wear"* *(Bereishis 28:20).*

Wake up and see the disadvantage of rushing to sustain your body. It will be with you for a limited time only; and during that time, it brings you nothing but grief. If it is fed too much, it becomes sick; if it is hungry it becomes weak. If you clothe it in too many garments, it is uncomfortable; if you dress it lightly, it suffers from the cold. Control of your body's health or sickness, life or death is not in your hands but in the Creator's, [so why work so hard for the sake of your body?]

The soul is much loftier than the body; it is rooted in a higher world. After death the soul ascends to God while the body descends to the earth. The soul is spiritual, whereas the body is physical; the soul is everlasting, whereas the body is temporary and disintegrates; the soul is elementary, while the body is complex; the soul is ethereal, while the body is crude; the soul has understanding, while the body's instinct is beastial; the soul inclines toward virtue, whereas the body leans toward loathsome traits.

If you are dedicated to preserve your lowly and flawed body, despite the fact that you are unable to help or harm it, surely you must dedicate yourself to the well-being of your exalted soul that lives on after your death. You were commanded to take care of it by acquiring wisdom and understanding, as it says, *"Purchase truth, do not sell it"* (Mishlei 23:23), *"Acquire wisdom, acquire under-standing"* (ibid. 4:5), and, *"How much better than fine gold is the ac-quisition of wisdom,* (ibid. 16:16); *"Eat honey, my child, for it is good . . . so is knowledge of wisdom to your soul"* (ibid. 24:14); and, *"If you have become wise, you have become wise for your own good"* (ibid. 9:12), which means that your spiritual assets are your own, and can never be taken from you; whereas your material possessions can be confiscated.

Contemplate on the differences between your body and soul and you will turn from this world, and work for your afterlife in the World to Come.

Don't say, "What happens to the fool will happen to me," [meaning, "on Judgment Day I will plead ignorance"], because you will be judged according to your [superior] knowledge, caus-ing your punishment to be severe and your excuse to be scrutinized rigorously. Don't assume that you can exonerate yourself with an excuse that has no merit, and don't try to offer an argument that will work against you.

It would take too long to explore this subject fully. The points I have made, should be sufficient for your level of understanding. Reflect on my words and try to understand what I am hinting at. Explore God's Torah and the words of our Sages, and you will find proof for my words in the Written and Oral Torah and by logic.

Using Your Intellect to Serve God

Thirteen: Given your knowledge and understanding, you should be doing more to serve God, to repay Him for all His favors.

Compare yourself to a servant whose master gave him a field to plant, with all the seed he needed. The servant planted only part of the field and used the rest of the seed for his own purposes. The master demanded an explanation and the servant admitted that he had not done his job properly. The master figured how much of the seed had been sown, calculated the expected yield [of the entire field], and made the servant pay not only for the seed he had taken but also for the crops the seed would have produced. As a result, the servant was punished doubly.

Apply the same calculation to yourself. God graciously granted you the ability to know Him and His Torah, and He gave you the means and the aptitude to fulfill your obligations to Him. Figure out how much of these obligations you have actually carried out. You will discover a shortfall, and you will be held accountable for what you owe. This is especially true when the Creator grants you special favors. So do your utmost to fulfill your obligations to the Creator. Bring your actions on par with your wisdom, and your efforts on par with your understanding.

Expend energy doing the mitzvos according to your wisdom. Don't waste your strength on the trivialities of this world, becoming too exhausted to fulfill the obligations of the Torah. God gave man the energy he needs to fulfill the Torah's obligations and to stay alive in this world; if you use your strength for nonessential things, you will not have it for worthwhile things.

Do not delude yourself saying, "If only I had a lot of money or were smarter, I would fulfill all my obligations to God." Such rationalizations are dishonest. You are deceiving yourself; if you rely on them you will stumble. This was the great mistake of the one with the "Security Mentality", [who demands a security from God before he is willing to serve Him, saying that he will start to serve God only after he has amassed enough capital for himself, his children and grandchildren,] as mentioned in the Gate of Trust. If you use this excuse, you are no better than all other sinners, and these alibis will not save you from punishment.

As Shlomoh said about thieves, *"A thief is not held in contempt for stealing to appease his hunger. Yet if caught, he must pay seven-fold"* (Mishlei 6:30,31). Even a needy thief forced by poverty to take other people's money, is not absolved from punishment. All the more so for sins [for which you have no excuse].

Seize the opportunity to meet your obligations to the Creator each day, and do not put off until tomorrow what you should do today, for tomorrow you may not be able to do it, even if you are alive. Worse yet, when the end of your life arrives, your excuses will be rejected and your explanations will evaporate. This world is like a marketplace where people assemble and then leave, where those who made a profit rejoice, and those who lose regret that they came. That is why the wise Shlomoh said, *"Remember your Creator in the days of your youth"* *(Koheles 12:1)*.

Awareness of God's Love

Fourteen: You feel love towards a person you think loves you, as it says, *"As water reflects face to face, so does one man's heart to another"* *(Mishlei 27:19)*. This is especially true if that person is a prince or a ruler. All the more so if he shows his love by wanting to be close to you, assuring you of his affection, offering you favors and being kind to you. Your love becomes so strong that nothing can deter it, and you would not spare any effort to do his bidding and serve him. You would place yourself, your possessions and your children at his disposal.

If this is the way you behave toward a frail mortal, how much more so are you obliged to your Creator, Who loves us, as it says, *"It was not because you had greater numbers than all the other nations that God preferred you and chose you . . . It was because of God's love for you"* *(Devarim 7:7)*. Besides declaring His love, His help is evident in the present and in the past and He has drawn us close to Him and promised to help us in every generation. As it says, *"Even when they are in their enemies' land, I will not grow so disgusted with them nor so tired of them that I would destroy them and break My covenant with them, since I am God their Lord"* *(Vayikra 26:44)*, and, *"For we are slaves [to the rulers of Persia], but even in our bondage God has not forsaken us"* *(Ezra 9:9)*.

We are obliged to remember the friendship shown to our father by respecting and loving his benefactor, as the wise Shlomoh said,

"Do not forsake your friend and the friend of your father" (*Mishlei 27:10*). God reminds us of the covenant He made with our ancestors; He watches over us for their sake, to keep His promise to them, as it says, *"Because He was keeping the oath that He made to your fathers"* (*Devarim 7:8*), and other verses to that effect.

One who does not trust in God and rely on His kindness, nor love Him, or devote himself to His service, and does not pour out his heart to Him in prayer, must be a very coarse and obstinate person whose faith is minimal and stubbornly resists the truth. He does not remember how much God loved his ancestors, and is not grateful for the love and protection God lavished on him.

He drew us close to Him and promised to help us always, yet we do not serve Him. He bestowed abundant kindness on us, yet we do not obey Him. He created us and guides us perfectly, yet we are unabashed.

Wake up from your sleep. Remove the curtain your *yetzer hara* has drawn to separate you from the light of reason. Your *yetzer hara* is a spider who weaves his web in a window. It becomes so opaque that sunlight cannot pass through. At first the threads of the web were delicate, but after a while they became thick enough to block the sunlight and prevent it from penetrating the house.

The *yetzer hara* also starts out weak, unable to prevent you from seeing the truth. If you detect it at this early stage, you can easily remove it from your heart. But if you do not pay attention, it grows stronger and will shut out the light of reason altogether. At that stage it is very difficult to banish it from your mind. Act quickly to save your soul, and pray to God that He help you drive out the *yetzer hara*. If you try hard [to overcome it], you will enjoy the light of wisdom, and you will see the truth.

Scripture alluded to the gradual takeover by the *yetzer hara* in the following verse, *"One day, a traveler came to a rich man, who was reluctant to take from his own sheep or cattle to prepare a meal for the guest who had come to him, so he took the poor man's lamb and prepared it for the man who had come to him"* (*2 Samuel 12:4*). The Sages (*Sukkah 52b*) note: First the *yetzer hara* is compared to "a traveler," then "a guest," and finally "a man".

In the same vein, it says, *"Happy is the man who has not walked in the counsel of the wicked, nor stood in the path of the sinners, nor sat the company of the insolent" (Tehillim 1:1)*. First [the *yetzer hara*] "walks by," then it "stands close" and finally it "sits" [and takes root in a person's heart]. There are many similar examples [that show how the *yetzer hara* gradually takes hold of a person's thoughts and actions, until it obscures the truth completely].

Analyze yourself on this score, and force yourself to do that which will save you. As the wise Shlomoh said about people who avoid thinking about such things, *"Evil men cannot understand judgment, but those who seek God understand everything" (Mishlei 28:5)*.

Prepare for Judgment Day

FIFTEEN: You stock up on food before you need it although you do not know whether you will live long enough to enjoy it. When you take a business trip, you make preparations well in advance, thinking about what merchandise is in demand there, how to get there, how much food to take along, who will travel with you, where you will stay, and the like, even though you do not know what fate God holds in store for you, or even if you will live to take the trip at all.

In the same manner, you should prepare for your final journey to the World to Come, a world from which there is no escape. Think about the provisions you must take with you, what [good deeds] you will have to offer the Creator on Judgment Day, which is described in the verse, *"Behold, that day is at hand, burning like an oven" (Malachi 3:19)*.

You are advancing constantly [toward the World to Come], but the road is long and the resting place [for the soul] is far away. You should be mindful of your destiny, and prepare the things you will need in your final home.

However, you concern yourself with this transitory world and leave the permanent world behind; you take care of your physical ailments and forget your spiritual afflictions. You serve your *yetzer hara* and forsake the service of God, you gratify your desires rather than serve your Creator.

Woe to us, that we live in such blinding confusion and miserable drunkenness, as it says, *"They have no wit or judgment: their eyes are besmeared from seeing, their minds from comprehending"* (*Yeshayah 44:18*), and, *"They are drunk, but not from wine, they stagger but not from liquor!"* (*ibid. 29:9*).

REFLECTIONS ON DEATH

SIXTEEN: Contemplate the length of your stay in this world, and the fact that the end is approaching. Death strikes people suddenly; it can come at any month, day, and hour, without distinction, to the elderly, the middle-aged, young adults, youths, children, and infants; it can happen any place, at any time.

It is as if a king deposited a sum of money with you, ordering you to expect him [to claim it] any time. You must be present when he comes, therefore you cannot possibly leave the place as long as you are holding the deposit.[1]

Or consider a debtor without a fixed due date. He expects his creditor to demand repayment at any time. Until he paid back the loan, he would have no peace of mind.

Many of your friends have preceded you to the other world, though they hoped to remain among the living. When you realize that you have done nothing to deserve longer life than they, you will scale down your worldly ambitions, and prepare for your after-life. You will focus on the provisions you must take with you on your journey to the hereafter, and make an accounting of yourself in anticipation of the Day of Reckoning.

---

1. The moral of the analogy is: God gave you a soul for safekeeping without telling you when to return it, so that you should always be ready for Him to come and claim it, and be mindful of it constantly (Marpe Lanefesh).

A Sage once said, "He who has placed death before him, has improved himself already." The wise Shlomoh said, *"The thoughts of the wise turn to the house of mourning"* (Koheles 7:4); *"It is better to go to the house of mourning than to the house of feasting, for that is the end of all man, and the living should take it to heart"* (ibid. 7:2). The living refers to people who are "spiritually alive," who have understanding and discernment. And it says, *"Man is like a breath"* (Tehillim 144:4).

REFRAINING FROM SOCIALIZING

SEVENTEEN: Be aware of the value of solitude and seclusion and the drawbacks to spending time needlessly with fools.

Some of the drawbacks include:

1. Fools utter senseless banalities, retelling over and over what "he said" or what "people say," and other such empty chatter. The wise Shlomoh said, *"When there is much talking, there is no lack of transgressing, but he who curbs his lips shows sense"* (Mishlei 10:19). A sage once said about this, "Hold on to your surplus words, and spend your surplus money [on charity]."

2. Fools slander other people, relating their faults and shameful acts. Scripture says about this, *"You sit and speak against your brother, you slander your mother's son"* (Tehillim 50:20).

3. Fools utter lies and falsehoods. Scripture says about this, *"Malice is within [the city], fraud and deceit never leave its square"* (ibid. 55:12); *"I have listened and heard: they do not speak honestly"* (Yirmeyah 8:6).

4. Fools swear falsely and without necessity. Concerning this, the Creator said, *"God will not allow the one who takes His Name in vain to go unpunished"* (Shemos 20:7). A pious man once said to his disciples, "The Torah permitted us to swear truthfully in God's Name. But I advise you not to swear by His Name [at all], either truthfully or falsely. Just say, "yes" or "no."

5. Fools boast and ridicule each other. I have explained in the

Gate of Humility why one should refrain from such conduct.

6. You will not be conscious of the fear of God while you associate with these people and talk with them.

7. Fools will inevitably cause you financial loss, because they talk about you [and your business dealings].

8. You will want to ingratiate yourself to these people, so you will brag about your expertise in the world of science—whether true or not.

9. You have the duty to urge these people to do good and to warn them against wrongdoing, as it says, *"Reprove your fellow"* (Vayikra 19:17).

You are required to warn against evil in three ways: by forcibly restraining them from sin, as Pinchas did when he saw Zimri committing a sin with Kosbi (Bamidbar 25:6-8); through admonition, as Moshe acted when he reproached the wicked man, saying, *"Why are you beating your brother?" (Shemos 2:13)*, and in your thoughts, as David did when he said, *"I detest the company of evil men, and do not consort with the wicked" (Tehillim 26:5)*.

When you see someone sinning, you must prevent him from sinning. Otherwise, you are guilty of ignoring the command to *"reprove your fellow"*. If you cannot stop him, you must at least protest verbally. If that too is impossible, fulfill the mitzvah in your thoughts, by hating the transgressor and keeping away from him.

If you associate with the masses, it is inevitable that you will have to take a stand against evildoers, because there are bound to be ignorant people who transgress. But if you live in seclusion, you are absolved from the obligation to command others to do good and to warn them against evil, which is a very difficult mitzvah to fulfill to perfection. As our Sages said, "I doubt that there is anyone in this generation who can accept reproof . . . and if there is anyone in this generation who knows how to reprove" (Arachin 16b).

10. By associating with frivolous people you lose your ability to think clearly. Your *yetzer hara* gathers strength, and you adopt their bad traits, as it says, *"He who befriends fools comes to grief" (Mishlei 13:20)*, and as our Sages said, "Children's chatter, and sitting in the meeting places of the ignorant, remove a person from the world" (Avos 3:10).

It takes two to commit most transgressions—including sexual immorality, fraudulent business dealings, false oaths, testifying falsely, and all transgression that are done through speech. Living in isolation saves you from these sins; it is the most effective way to acquire good character traits. The Sages agree that the mainstay of purity of heart is the love of solitude. Do not allow the *yetzer hara* make socializing seem appealing to you and make you yearn for it when you are alone.

SOLITUDE IS GOOD; BEFRIENDING SAGES IS BETTER

Befriending sages who know God and His Torah, is even better than isolating oneself from society. [The purpose of isolation is to keep you from the influence of frivolous people, so that you can concentrate on serving God;] being close to righteous men and Torah scholars is far more effective than isolation in achieving this goal. The wise Shlomoh said, "*He who keeps company with the wise becomes wise, but he who befriends fools comes to grief*" *(Mishlei 13:20)*; "*Incline your ear and listen to the words of the sages*" *(ibid. 22:17)*. A person who does not befriend kindhearted people is described in the verse, "*The scoffer dislikes being reproved, he will not go to the sages*" *(Mishlei 15:12)*. Our Sages said on this subject, "A gathering of wicked people is bad for them and bad for the world, whereas a gathering of righteous people is good for them and good for the world; the scattering of wicked people is good for them and good for the world, the scattering of the righteous is bad for them and bad for the world" (Sanhedrin 71b) and, "Let your house be a meeting place for sages, sit in the dust of their feet, and drink their words thirstily" (Avos 1:4), and it says, "*Then those who fear God spoke to one another, and God listened and heard*" *(Malachi 3:16)*.

BE HUMBLE AND GRATEFUL TO GOD

EIGHTEEN: When you feel yourself becoming arrogant, craving positions of honor in this world, compare your worth to the higher and lower beings, and you will realize how insignificant you are among God's creations, as I explained in the Gate of Humility.

Then consider the eminence God has granted man; letting him dominate animals, plants, and minerals, as it says, *"You have made him master over Your handiwork, laying the world at his feet"* *(Tehillim 8:7)*. God also let man know the laws of the Torah, and gave him insight into the mysteries of the upper and lower regions of the universe, for his benefit.

God has greatly elevated us, allowing us to praise and thank Him, and to appeal to Him in times of trouble, and by answering our prayers. He further exalted us, choosing prophets to whom He revealed the mysteries of His might and through whom He performed miracles. In addition, He bestowed on us innumerable hidden and apparent favors—both physical and spiritual—some affecting many people, others touching individuals.

Though you are insignificant God has exalted you—this, despite the fact that He does not need you, yet you sorely need His providence. Be considerate of the glorious crown God placed on you, of the lofty status He has granted you in this world, and the great reward He has set aside for you in the World to Come, by dedicating yourself to His service and showing your gratitude.

Do not become arrogant and overbearing. Do not think that you deserve your lofty status. Be submissive instead, seeing how lowly you actually rank in God's creation.

Act like a lowly servant would act, if his master promoted him to his inner circle. He would humbly maintain the demeanor he had before his master favored him. He would not act proudly in front of his master, nor be conceited because of the prominence he has won. He would not make requests of his master in a nonchalant manner [as if he deserved fulfillment of his wishes]. Instead, he would leave his concerns with his master, trusting him.

A certain *tzaddik* added to his *Shemoneh esrei* the following: "God, I am taking the liberty to stand before You, not out of ignorance of my own lowliness or unawareness of Your greatness and exaltedness. I know that You are sublime and uplifted, and I am too lowly, despicable and insignificant to ask anything from You, to praise You or sanctify Your holy Name, the way the holy angels sanctify You. I am taking the liberty to do this, because You commanded me to pray to You and permitted me to praise You to the best of my ability, and because I want to demonstrate my service and humility to you.

"I let You know my needs, not because I want to persuade You to fulfill them. After all, You know what is best for me, and how I should conduct myself [to avoid getting hurt]. I only express my needs in order to make myself mindful of my dependence on You, and my trust in You. If, in my ignorance, I have asked You for something that is not good and beneficial for me, please do not fulfill my request, but do what You judge to be best for me, because what Your exalted choice sets aside for me is better than what I would choose for myself. Therefore, I leave all my concerns to Your immutable decision and Your sublime guidance. As David said, *"O God, my heart is not proud nor my look haughty; I do not aspire to great things nor to what is beyond me. I swear that I stilled and silenced my soul, like a suckling child at his mother's side, like the suckling child am I in my mind"* (Tehillim 131:1).

GOD SPARED YOU ALTHOUGH YOU SINNED

NINETEEN: The Creator has spared you from misfortune and distress, from rampant diseases and hardships like imprisonment, hunger, thirst, cold, heat, poisoning, attacks by wild animals, leprosy, insanity and stroke. God protects you from adversity, although you deserve these affliction as punishment for the sins you have committed before the Creator. These include rebellious acts, contempt of His word, failure to thank, praise and serve Him, failure to repent and confess your sins, and defying God over a long period of time despite the fact that He showered you with goodness and kindness throughout that time.

When you consider how the Creator has tested mankind with adversity yet spared you, you will praise God for the great kindness He has shown you. You will ask forgiveness for past transgressions for which God has shown forbearance and not punished you. You will devote yourself to the service of God to ward off these afflictions, as it says, *"If you obey God your Lord and do what is upright in His eyes, carefully heeding all His commandments and keeping all His decrees, then I will not strike you with any of the sicknesses that I brought on Egypt for I am God Who heals you" (Shemos 15:26)*; and it says, *"If only you obey these laws . . . God will take all sickness from you. He will not allow any of the terrible Egyptian afflictions to affect you" (Devarim 7:15)*. As one of our early pious men said to his disciples, "You see, it is not the snake that kills, but the sin!" (Berachos 33a), and it says, *"You will tread on cubs and vipers; you will trample lions and serpents; [God says:] For he has yearned for Me I will deliver him; I will elevate him, because he knows My Name" (Tehillim 91:13)*.

REFLECTING ON HOW YOU USE YOUR MONEY

TWENTY: If you have acquired capital, account for your resources. How did you acquire your capital? Are you spending it on your obligations to God and to others as you should? Your money is not exclusively yours forever; remember that it is left with you as a deposit for as long as the Creator wishes, and He will give it to someone else when He wants to. Think like this, and you will not constantly worry about losing your fortune. You will be grateful to God if your money remains with you; if you lose it, you will accept His decree. It will be easy to spend it in the service of God, to do good with it, and return what has been entrusted to you or what has been fraudulently obtained. You will not envy another person's wealth, nor look down on poor people. In fact, [when you recognize that your wealth is only on deposit with you,] your money will become an inducement for acquiring good qualities and giving up objectionable ones. For it says, *"Honor God with your wealth"* (*Mishlei 3:9*), and, *"He who is generous to the poor makes a loan to God. He will repay him his due"* (*ibid. 19:17*).

ACTUALIZE YOUR POTENTIAL

TWENTY-ONE: Determine the highest level of service to God you are capable of reaching. Do whatever you can, eagerly and diligently, until it becomes a habit. Make it your goal to do more than you seem capable of doing. Set your heart on attaining it, and ask God sincerely to give you the fortitude to do more than you seem capable of doing.

If you do this continually, the Creator will fulfill your wish and open the gates of knowledge of Him. Bit by bit He will strengthen your mind and your limbs and enable you to fulfill those mitzvos that are now beyond your reach, as it says, *"Thus says God your Redeemer, 'I am the Lord your God instructing you for your own benefit, guiding you in the way you should go'"* (*Yeshayah 48:17*).

This can be compared to one learning a trade. When he starts, he does as much as he can at the time, which is less than what he is actually capable of. As his skill improves, the Creator reveals to him the underlying principles of the trade, and he discovers new techniques.

The same goes for the sciences. A teacher of geometry cannot teach his student theoretical geometry at first. He begins by teaching him practical geometry using the geometric figures that Euclid used in his works on the subject. When the student grasps practical geometry and diligently tries to make new deductions, the Creator reveals theoretical geometry to him, and strengthens his knowledge of the subject so that he can construct magnificent figures and subtle designs that are almost akin to God-given prophetic revelations.[2]

---

2. This is apparent today when we see how *baalei teshuvah* who have no prior knowledge of Judaism, with special *siyata diShmaya* [Divine assistance], become proficient in Gemara and Halachah on par with advanced Talmudic scholars within just a few short years.

The same goes for other sciences as well. A hard working student will be stimulated by a supernatural power that no human being could have given him. Our Sages had this in mind when they said, "A wise man is superior to a prophet" (Bava Basra 12a). And Elihu [one of Iyov's companions] said, *"But truly it is a spirit in man, it is the soul from the Almighty, that gives him understanding"* (Iyov 32:8).

Based on this analogy, understand that the main purpose of the physical mitzvos [like tefillin and sukkah], is to encourage us to fulfill the mitzvos of the heart [like believing in God, trusting Him, loving Him, and loving one's neighbor]. These are the cornerstone of service to God and the foundation of the Torah, as it says, *"Be in awe of God and serve Him"* (Devarim 10:20); *"[The Torah] is something that is very close to you. It is in your mouth and in your heart, so that you can keep it"* (ibid. 30:14), and, *"What does God want of you? Only that you remain in awe of God"* (ibid. 10:12).

The mitzvos of the heart are beyond human capacity, and one cannot fulfill them without shaking off most of his animal desires, controlling his instincts, and keeping a tight rein on his movements. Therefore, the Creator gave us mitzvos which we are capable of performing, mitzvos done with our body and limbs, which make it easier to fulfill the mitzvos of the heart.

When you strive to fulfill the mitzvos of the heart, God opens the gate of spiritual excellence for you, so that you can attain spiritual heights ordinarily beyond your reach, and thereby you will serve the Creator with body and soul, outwardly and inwardly. As David said, *"My body and soul shout for joy to the living God"* (Tehillim 84:3).

This is like a man who planted trees, pulled the weeds around them, cleared the soil of thorns and stubble, and watered and fertilized the trees. Then he can hope that they will bear fruit. But if he neglects the trees, he does not deserve fruit from God.

The same is true of your service to God. If you zealously do the best you can, God will help you do things normally beyond your capacity. This is the most precious fruit that God gives to His chosen people in this world, as our Sages said, "Whoever fulfills the Torah in poverty, [i.e. with insufficient knowledge], will ultimately fulfill it in wealth [i.e. rich in wisdom]" (Avos 4:9). The wise Shlomoh said, *"To the man who pleases Him, He has given wisdom, knowledge and joy" (Koheles 2:26)*. And our Sages said (Avodah Zarah 20b), "Torah study leads to action, action leads to alertness, alertness leads to diligence, diligence leads to abstinence, abstinence leads to innocence, innocence leads to piety, and piety is the greatest quality of them all, for it says, *"Then You spoke in a vision to Your devout one" (Tehillim 89:20)*.

If you neglect your duties and underestimate your abilities, God will not support you in your service to Him, as it says, *"God is far from the wicked" (Mishlei 15:29)*, and, *"Your iniquities have been a barrier between you and your God" (Yeshayah 59:2)*.

THE IMPORTANCE OF ACQUIRING GOOD FRIENDS

TWENTY-TWO: You do many things together with others that benefit the world, like plowing, harvesting, buying and selling. Do you want others to have the things you want to have? Are you unhappy when things you would not want happening to you, happen to them? Do you treat your fellows with compassion and prevent hurtful things from happening to them, as it says, *"Love your fellow as yourself" (Vayikra 19:18)*?

We can compare this to people traveling to a faraway country on a difficult road having to spend many nights in lodges. There were few people, yet each had many heavily-laden animals with him, which had to be loaded and unloaded. If they help each other load and unload, each caring for the well-being of the group and equally sharing the work, they will be all right. But if each one thinks only of himself, most of them will not make it.

So too in the world at large, because everyone thinks only of himself wanting a bigger share than God allotted him, life is troublesome for most people, and people must work hard for a living. Since everyone demands more than his share seeking things that do not belong to them, they cannot obtain even the share allotted to them. As a result, people are not satisfied with what they have. Because they demand luxuries, the world denies them the essentials, forcing them to go to great trouble to obtain the things they want.

If people were satisfied with the essentials and would help each other, they would overcome all obstacles and have more than they hoped to achieve. But unfortunately they do not help each other; rather, they hinder each other, and sap each other's strength. Thus no one reaches his goal.

If you acquire faithful friends they will help you advance in your Torah studies and in your worldly pursuits. How can you find such friends? By being devoted to them. If you find friends worthy of your trust, hold them as dear as yourself. But do not reveal your secrets to anyone but your closest friend, as Ben Sira (6:6) said, *"Though many may wish you well, reveal your secrets to but one in a thousand."* And the wise Shlomoh said, *"Oil and incense gladden the heart, and the sweetness of a friend's [advice] is better than your own counsel"* (Mishlei 27:9).

DON'T TAKE GOD'S CREATION FOR GRANTED

TWENTY-THREE: The wonders of God's creation are evident in the world around you, from the smallest to the largest creatures. Reflect about man's superiority over everything, about the relative standing of lower and higher beings [i.e angels]; about the orbits of the heavenly bodies, about the movements of the sun, the moon, the constellations and the stars; about rainfall, wind, the way a baby is born, and about things that are even more wondrous, subtle, obvious yet mysterious, among the marvels of God's creation, which testify to His perfect wisdom and power, His beneficial guidance, His all-encompassing compassion and mercy, and the way He oversees all His creatures.

Do not become indifferent because you have seen these phenomena every day since you were a child. Do not let your knowledge of these sights make you take them for granted.

Both common people and distinguished persons have this attitude. They are overwhelmed by the things they see rarely, like an eclipse of the sun or the moon, lightning, thunder, an earthquake, hurricanes, and the like, but they are not impressed by the revolutions and orbits of the sun, the moon and the stars, by sunrises and sunsets, rainfall, wind, and other daily occurrences. They are amazed when they see the ocean with its waves and storms and the multitude of creatures in it, but the flow and incessant gushing of water from springs leaves them cold.

Don't adopt this mental outlook. It is important to reflect on everything God created, whether you are familiar with it or not. You turned a blind eye to the wonders of nature when you first saw them as a child. Don't let this mistake keep you from contemplating them now that you are an adult with mature intellect and keen insight.

Observe them now as if you had never seen them before. Pretend that you were blind, and your eyes have just opened. An ignorant man is like a blind man; when he understands something he is like a person whose eyes have been opened. As the verse says about Adam and Eve, *"The eyes of both of them were opened"* *(Bereishis 3:7)*, we know, of course, that their eyes were already open; [but they gained a new insight and realized].

If you study natures phenomena you will discover their essence, and recognize the Creator's wonders of which you were so ignorant. As a wise man once said, "The hearts of sages have eyes that see what fools cannot." And as Scripture says, *"Do you not know? Have you not heard? Have you not been told from the very first? Have you not contemplated how the earth was founded? . . . Lift high your eyes and see: Who created these? (Yeshayah 40:21).*

SHED YOUR PRECONCEIVED NOTIONS

TWENTY-FOUR: Reassess your ideas about God and His Torah, the teachings and parables of the early rabbinic sages and the meanings of the various prayers you learned as a child when you first went to school. [Study these concepts from your present mature perspective,] for the undeveloped mind cannot understand subtle concepts as clearly as the mature intellect can. The more you grow intellectually, the better you understand these ideas.

Do not rely on the notions you embraced when you first began to learn about difficult problems. With your more mature point of view, look afresh at the Torah and the Prophets and study them as if you had never read them before. Explain and comment on them, explore the exact wording, sentence structure, and various interpretations of the verses. Weigh which passages can be interpreted according to their plain meaning, and which cannot, which can be understood and which are beyond human comprehension, which passages have parallel references in Scripture and which do not.

Do the same with prayers and hymns; examine their words and underlying meaning, so that you will know what you are saying and asking for, when you recite your prayers before God. Do not run through your prayers without understanding them and without paying attention to them as children do. We have already elaborated on this enough.

Delve into the words of the Sages and the Oral Torah. When something baffles you, blame it on your lack of understanding. Demand of yourself that you study like a beginner. Impress that which you do understand on your mind and commit it to memory. That which you are unsure of, ask the sages of your generation and they will help you. As long as you don't research it the way you did as a youngster, the secrets of the Torah, the Prophets and the Sages will be revealed to you with a degree of clarity you could never have attained from your first teachers.

Do not be arrogant, thinking there is nothing left to learn, and never changing your youthful opinions. The *yetzer hara* is trapping you, by keeping you from exploring, and convincing you that you are an accomplished sage. As the wise Shlomoh said, *"The lazy man thinks himself wiser than seven men who give good advice"* (Mishlei 26:16); *"If you see a man who thinks himself wise, there is more hope for a fool than for him"* (ibid. 26:12). And it says also, *"A wise man has his eyes towards his beginnings"* (Koheles 2:14), meaning, a wise man examines his old ideas of Torah and worldly concerns and sifts the good from the bad. He then continues to do good and repents of the bad, while a fool disdains all that.

A fool is compared to a person who travels a long road in the dark of night, never looking back. Even were he to look back, he would not see anything, therefore his mind lies only on what is ahead. That is why Shlomoh said, *"A fool walks in darkness"* (ibid.), and, *"I found that wisdom is superior to folly as light is superior to darkness"* (ibid. v 13).

SPIRITUAL PURSUITS VERSUS BODILY NEEDS

TWENTY-FIVE: You have become preoccupied with this world, placing its pleasures ahead of the World to Come. Dislodge the love of this world from your heart, replacing it with the love of the World to Come by comparing your destiny in both worlds.

Concentrate on loving the World to Come always, which will dislodge love of this world from your mind; for the two cannot exist side by side. As a sage once said, "Just as water and fire cannot co-exist in the same vessel, so too, love of this world and love of the World to Come cannot exist together in the heart of a believer," and furthermore, "This world and the World to Come are like two wives of the same husband: please one, the other gets angry."

Both your body and soul need care. You strengthen your soul by adhering to the rules of ethics and the study of Torah, by giving it wise guidance and teaching it good character traits, and by curbing its sensual desires. You strengthen your body by providing it with nutritious food, with healthful drinks, by bathing in warm water, and by taking care of its needs.

If you attend to your body alone, you will neglect enrichment of your soul; and if you focus on the soul alone, you will neglect the needs of your body. Give priority to your immortal soul, but at the same time, do not neglect your bodily needs. If you neglect your body, you will sap its strength, thereby weakening both body and soul. Provide your body with the basic food it needs, but provide your soul with even more wisdom than you think it can absorb. The wise Shlomoh said in this regard, *"Don't be overly righteous or excessively wise. Why be left desolate? Don't be overly wicked, and don't be a fool, or you may die before your time. . . It is best that you grab the one without letting go of the other"* (Koheles 7:16-18). That is, do not seclude yourself from the world. And do not attach greater importance to this world than the next. Do not satisfy desires that are not required for your Torah observance and for staying alive in this world. The phrase, *"You may die before your time"* means your soul may perish when your lust gains the upper hand, drowning your soul in a flood of sensual pleasure.

Think about the World to Come, but do not withdraw from this world, because you must take the provisions you need for the hereafter from this world. As our Sages said, "This world is like a lobby before the world to come. Prepare yourself in the lobby so that you may enter the banquet hall" (Avos 4:16). This was the way of life of the early God-fearing pious people.

The reason that King Shlomoh said, *"Don't be overly wise"* but did not say, *"Don't be overly foolish,"* is, because we cannot pursue wisdom limitlessly. You are permitted, even required, to pursue any kind of wisdom that induces you to serve God and to keep His mitzvos, and that manifests His wisdom and power. As it says, *"See, fear of God is wisdom"* (Iyov 28:28); *" The beginning of wisdom is the fear of God, and the [beginning of] understanding is knowledge of the Holy One"* (Mishlei 9:10). *"The beginning of wisdom is the fear of God"* (Tehillim 111:10); *"The wise shall be put to shame, they shall be dismayed and caught; see they reject the word of God, so their wisdom amounts to nothing"* (Yirmeyah 8:9). But we may not explore any branch of wisdom that is not conducive to the fear of God, the observance of mitzvos, or recognition of God's wisdom and power. Therefore it says, *"Don't be overly wise,"* [meaning, indeed study but refrain from subjects that are forbidden].

But all foolishness is reprehensible. That is why Shlomo said, *"Don't be a fool"* rather than, *"Don't be overly foolish,"* because even the least bit of foolishness ruins many good qualities, as it says,

"Dead flies putrefy the perfumer's oil; a little folly outweighs wisdom and honor" (Koheles 10:1).

A PARADOX: FEARING A HUMAN RULER MORE THAN GOD

TWENTY-SIX: You obey an order of a king and fear to violate it, yet you are unimpressed by God's commandments and are not afraid of being punished for transgressing them.

There is a vast difference between the command of the Creator and that of a mortal king. A mortal king is incapable of enforcing his decrees, is slow to punish transgressors, is far from you and cannot see you all the time and is too involved in his own business to care about you. Yet in spite of all this, the wise Shlomoh said, *"Fear God, my son, and [respect] the king" (Mishlei 24:21)*, and, *"The terror of a king is like the roar of a young lion" (ibid. 20:2)*. Surely an intelligent person must be ashamed before God, Whose decrees are everlasting, Who gazes at you all the time, and Who cannot be distracted or prevented from doing as He pleases.

How can you not fear Him and His punishment? How dare you rebel against His word, knowing that He watches you and examines you inside and out? Do not delay repenting of your shortcomings. Say to yourself, "I have rebelled against His word for so long, and He still has not punished me. Let me ask His forgiveness before He obliterates me in this world and punishes me in the World to Come". As David says, *"The wicked man, arrogant as he is, in all his scheming thinks, 'He will not avenge; there is not God'" (Tehillim 10:4)*.

WHATEVER GOD DECIDES IS FOR THE BEST

TWENTY-SEVEN: When bad things occur, affecting either your health, your finances or another aspect of your life, realize that whatever God allots is for the best. Accept your plight willingly rather than being resentful, as it says, *"So I will wait for God, Who is hiding His face from the house of Jacob, and I will trust Him"* *(Yeshayah 8:17)*. Don't be like one about whom it says, *"When he is hungry, he will be[come] angry and curse his king and his gods, and [only then will he] direct his face [to God] on high"* *(ibid. v. 21)*.[3]

We praise our forefather Abraham for passing his ten God given trials because he accepted them willingly, with a cheerful heart, as it says, *"You found his heart true to You"* *(Nechemiah 9:8)*. The generation of the Exodus were chastised in the wilderness when they were angry with God and did not accept Him and His prophet Moshe cheerfully as it says, *"They deceived Him with their speech, lied to Him with their words; their hearts were not honest with Him"* *(Tehillim 78:36)*. Indeed, they rebelled against God, defied His word, and broke His covenant many times by longing to return to Egypt whenever something annoyed them.

If you accept suffering willingly, it will ultimately bring you good things, but if you accept suffering grudgingly, you receive neither reward nor forgiveness for transgressions. Note that the two ways of reacting to suffering, bring opposite results.

There are three types of suffering: A person may take it upon himself to suffer, [like fasting, and ascetic practices] as a way of serving God; or he may suffer by abstaining from things that would provoke God, [like forbidden sensual pleasures]; or he may suffer personal misfortune. The last kind of suffering can be subdivided into two categories: suffering because you lack basic necessities, or because you don't have an item you always wanted though you can do without it.

The last two categories of suffering are inflicted on you either as punishment to atone for transgressions, or as a trial and test, in order to increase your reward [when you pass].

Whether suffering comes as a punishment or as a test, accept it gladly as God's will. As David said, *"All the ways of God are kindness and truth to those who guard His covenant and testimonies"*

[3.] When he realizes that his king and his gods cannot save him, he will look to Heaven and pray to the true God.

(Tehillim 25:10). [The passage speaks of "kindness" and "truth,"] for if God brought suffering on you to atone for transgressions, your suffering falls under the category of "truth," [for you truly deserve it,] and if He caused you to suffer as a test, in order to reward you when you pass, your suffering is a "kindness" from God.

When you realize that all forms of suffering are for your own good, your adversity will benefit you, and your reward for it is assured. You will be strong enough to reconcile yourself to any misfortune that God may send your way, and your heartache will be soothed. You show thereby that you accept God's decree willingly, taking solace in Him, and placing your trust in Him, as it says, *"Be strong, and let your hearts take courage, all who wait longingly for God"* *(Tehillim 31:25)*.

TRUST GOD, EVEN WHEN BAD THINGS HAPPEN

TWENTY-EIGHT: Do not complain if you entrusted your life, your property, your children and everything else to the Creator and then your situation takes a turn for the worse. Compare your situation with one who gave his friend a house as a gift. Then the recipient tore down the house and rebuilt it in a different style. Can the donor be upset at the way his friend remodeled the house? After all, he gave the house as a gift!

So too, if you willingly entrusted your life and possessions to God, do not complain when He treats you the way He wants to, even if it does not seem to be to your benefit. Rather, accept what He does, and rely on His superior judgment.

Do not regret that you gave Him what you thought was yours, and do not be distraught at His decree. Remember, you are one of His creations; He formed, sustained and guided you for your own good, both in your outer and inner concerns, even though you do not understand that this is so. As it says, *"I sent [a leader] to Ephraim who took them upon his arms, and they did not know that I healed them "* *(Hoshea 11:3)*.

Your Soul Ranks Higher than Your Body

Twenty-nine: Your soul ranks higher than your body. Some people are worth more than others. In fact, one person may be worth as much as a thousand people. But this superiority is derived only from spiritual qualities, not due to physical strength, as David's warriors said to David, [because of his inner worth] *"Now you are worth ten thousand of us"* (2 Shmuel 18:3).

Even a woman of outstanding beauty looks unattractive if she lacks inner grace and nobility, as the wise Shlomoh said, *"Like a gold ring in the snout of a pig, is a beautiful woman bereft of sense"* (Mishlei 11:22), and, *"Grace is deceptive, beauty is illusory. It is for her fear of God that a woman is to be praised"* (ibid. 31:30).

The more you are aware of the soul's superiority over the body, the more you will try to enhance your soul [by doing good deeds], protecting it from punishment from its Master, Who observes whether it is pure or soiled, praiseworthy or loathsome, whether it chooses good or evil and whether it leans toward reason or lust.

Care for your soul more than for your body. It is easier to cure your body of the most dangerous disease than to heal your soul of the disease it catches when the *yetzer hara* takes possession of it. As the wise Shlomoh said, *"A man's spirit will sustain him through any illness, but low spirits—who can bear them?"* (Mishlei 18:14), and, *"More than all that you guard, guard your mind"* (ibid. 4:23).

Consider Yourself A Foreigner

The thirtieth and final way of introspection: Assess whether you consider yourself an alien in this world. Imagine a stranger arriving in a foreign country. The ruler, feeling sorry for the despondent stranger, helped him adjust to his new surroundings. He provided him with his daily needs, only asking in return that he abide by his laws. He promised reward for his obedience, and threatened punishment if he violated his laws.

The ruler told him to always be prepared to leave the country, though he did not specify a departure time. While residing in the country, though, he stipulated things the stranger must do.

The stranger is obligated to be humble and cast off arrogance, as it says, *"This man came here as an immigrant, and now, all of a sudden, he has set himself up as a judge!" (Bereishis 19:9).*

He must be prepared to leave at any time, and not plan to take up permanent residence, as it says, *"Since the land is Mine, no land shall be sold permanently. You are foreigners and resident aliens as far as I am concerned" (Vayikra 25:23).*

He must study the laws of the country and his obligations to the king, as David said, *"I am only a sojourner in the land; do not hide Your commandments form me" (Tehillim 119:19).*

He must love other foreigners like he loves himself, helping them, as it says, *"You must show love toward the foreigner" (Devarim 10:19),* and, *"The foreigner who resides with you must be exactly like one who is native-born among you; you shall love him as [you love] yourself" (Vayikra 19:34).*

He must energetically perform service to the government, because no one will pity him if he is lax about performing his service. His situation is opposite that of the Shunamite woman. For when the prophet Elisha asked her, *"Can we speak on your behalf to the king or to the army commander? She replied, "I live among my own people" (2 Melachim 4:13),* meaning, "My people and my family will speak to him on my behalf, when needed". The situation of the foreigner is altogether different, as David put it, *"Look at my right and see—I have no friend; there is nowhere I can flee, no one cares about me" (Tehillim 142:5).*

He should be satisfied with the food, shelter and clothing he can find, living frugally. He should think about his upcoming journey and prepare the provisions he will need for the way.

He should appreciate even the smallest favor he receives, expressing profuse thanks to whomever was kind to him.

He should patiently resign himself to any misfortune that may strike him. Being depressed will not help, since he cannot prevent calamities from happening.

You too, should act like a foreigner in this world, since in essence you are one. The proof of this lies in the fact that when you were born, no one could hasten or delay the moment of your birth by a fraction of a minute, could attach or detach one limb from another, create any of your internal or external organs, make an immobile part of your body mobile, or visa versa or make your delivery in this world easier or more difficult.

After you were born, no one could feed you without God's help, or make you taller or shorter than you are. Even were you to be the only person in the world, your income would not grow by as much as a mustard seed's worth beyond what was assigned to you. Conversely, if the world population would be many times its present size, your income would not shrink by as much as a mustard seed beyond what you were allotted. You will get what you are destined to have—no more, no less. No one can help or harm you, prolong or shorten your life [without God's consent]. The same goes for all your character traits, qualities and achievements, good or bad.

In light of the fact that you are an alien in this world, what relationship is there between you and the other beings in the world? In reality, you are nothing but a stranger in the world. It would not help you if there were more people in the world; it would not hurt you if there were only few. You are but a solitary individual, whose only companion is his Master, with no friend that feels for him except his Creator.

Therefore, devote yourself entirely to His service, just as He devoted Himself to creating and nurturing you, with your life and death entirely in His hands. Be mindful of His Written and Oral Torah. Hope for reward from Him and fear His punishment. Consider yourself a foreigner in this world as I mentioned earlier. If you do, you will enjoy the bliss of the World to Come, as the wise Shlomoh said, *"Know: such is wisdom for your soul; if you attain it there is a future; your hope will not be cut off"* (Mishlei 24:14).

SUMMARY

These are the thirty points to consider, when you engage in serious introspection before God. Face yourself honestly and their light will break through to you. Keep them in mind, reflecting on them as long as you live.

Do not be satisfied with the few things I discussed and with my brief outline of the thirty points. Each theme, contains many more details than I have mentioned. I merely aroused your interest by offering you tidbits. I did not elaborate on the themes, so that the book would not become too long, for my original intention was only to whet the reader's appetite.

Be mindful of these thirty points and each time you review them you will discover ethical teachings you did not see before. Do not think that by arriving at the superficial meaning of the words you have unraveled their inner meaning. You will accomplish that only after long and diligent reflection.

Correct yourself and others by means of these thirty ways, and you will earn God's greatest reward, as it says, *"The knowledgeable will be radiant like the bright expanse of the sky, and those that lead the many to righteousness will be like the stars for ever and ever"* *(Daniel 12:3)*, and the wise Shlomoh said, *"Those who admonish will delight"* *(Mishlei 24:25)*.

CHAPTER FOUR

The Benefits of Introspection

———⟨◉⟩———

The benefits of introspection are seen in the soul when it grasps the thirty ways of self-analysis, understands their essence, and realizing that they are necessary, eagerly takes them upon itself. The better the soul understands the thirty ways, the more eager it is to engage in them.

Do this and you will sense an exciting inner renewal and learn good character traits. You will attain precious qualities, clearing your soul of folly, and driving away doubt that fills your heart.

In research, the more convincing, logical and numerous the hypotheses, the more significant and clear are the results. The same goes for mixing medicinal compounds: the more potent the ingredients, the more effective the drug. This is true also for mathematics: the more solid the propositions for a given theorem, the stronger the proof.

Many other things are like that too. You cannot build a scale unless you know something about mathematics and the properties of weights and measures. You cannot put together an astrolabe unless you have mastered mathematics, geometry, astronomy and geography.

And the same goes for your soul. It cannot reach its full potential unless you do the soul-searching you were encouraged to do in this and other Gates.

Do this faithfully and your mind will become crystal clear. You will reach the loftiest levels, with the *yetzer hara* unable to entice you. You will be among God's treasured ones, and a peculiar metaphysical power that you never knew before, will emerge in you, as the wise Shlomoh said, *"A man's wisdom lights up his face, and the boldness of his face is transformed"* (Koheles 8:1).

You will perceive marvelous things, fathoming profound mysteries, because your soul is cleansed, your heart pure, and your faith strong. You will enjoy everlasting happiness in this world and the next, because of the spectacular insights you have gained and the sublime mystery that will be revealed to you, with God's help.

Imagine standing in a room, with an exquisite object above the ceiling that you would like to see. The opening in the ceiling is not placed properly to see the object. If you took a metal plate, ground it down until it was smooth, polished it with a buffing compound until it shone like a mirror and then placed it in front of your face, you would be able to see the object and enjoy its delicate form and enchanting beauty.

The impressive figure that you cannot see represents the Creator's wisdom and power and the beauty of the heavenly world whose form and essence are hidden from us. The metal plate stands for the human soul; the polishing of the plate represents your study of Torah-based wisdom and ethics. The buffing compound symbolizes the thirty ways of introspection.

When you etch them into your thoughts, your soul will become pure and your mind crystal clear. You will perceive supernatural concepts and understand the true nature of things. The gate to higher wisdom will be opened, and the curtain separating you from the Creator's wisdom will be lifted. God will teach you metaphysical wisdom and the performance of propitious deeds.

God will then give you divine inspiration, as it says, *"The spirit of God will rest upon him, a spirit of wisdom and insight, a spirit of counsel and strength, a spirit of knowledge and fear of God"* (Yeshayah 11:2), and, *"But truly it is the spirit of man, and it is the soul from the Almighty that gives them understanding"* (Iyov 32:8), and, *"If you seek it as you do silver, and search for it as for treasures, then you will understand the fear of God and attain knowledge of God"* (Mishlei 2:4,5).

CHAPTER FIVE

MUST ONE ENGAGE IN INTROSPECTION ALL THE TIME?

———◦◉◦———

One must engage in introspection constantly. Thereby the fear of God Who watches you all the time will never leave you.

This can be inferred from God's commandment to the Jewish king, for it says, *"[The king] must write a copy of this Torah as a scroll before the Levite priests. [This scroll] must always be with him, and he shall read from it all the days of his life"* (Devarim 17:18). So too God said to Yehoshua, *"Let not this Book of the Torah depart from your mouth; rather you should contemplate it day and night"* (Yehoshua 1:8). And, *"These words which I am commanding you today must remain on your heart* (Devarim 6:6), and, *"Bind these words as a sign on your hand, and let them be an emblem in the center of your head. Also write them on [parchments affixed to] the doorposts of your house and gates"* (ibid. v. 8). This obligation is stressed in connection with the mitzvah of *tzitzis*, for it says, *"These shall be your tzitzis, and when you see them, you shall remember all of God's commandments so as to keep them"* (Bamidbar 15:39,40).

God did not overlook any method capable of encouraging us toward introspection. Therefore you must make a self-assessment at all times. Do not underrate the value of any good thing you do for His sake, even if it is only a word or a glance. What seems insignificant to you, is important to Him. The same is true for transgressions. The closest analogy to this is the movement of the sun.

When it seems from earth to move the distance of a cubit, it is actually moving many miles. The same goes for the movement of the shadow on an astrolabe.

At the same time, do not overrate your good deeds, even if you did them for the sake of God. With an accurate accounting you will find that just a few of the favors God has done for you outweigh by far all the good done by the population of the whole world.

Assess where you stand in relation to your Creator, in light of His great favors to you, and His many daily acts of kindness. If you are unable to do so in the daytime, do it at night, and if you miss a day, make up for it the next day. As our Sages said, "Repent one day before your death" (Avos 2:10), and it says, *"Let your garments always be white" (Koheles 9:8)*.

CHAPTER SIX

THE COURSE OF ACTION TO TAKE
FOLLOWING INTROSPECTION

——◦◦◉◦◦——

If your soul is pure and is receptive to the lights of truth coming to it from God, you will be objective in your self-analysis, understand its intentions, and do it for the sake of God. Then God will be pleased with you, and will help you fulfill His mitzvos, teaching you to see the truth which casts out all doubts, and filling you with the light of wisdom which will purify you inside and out. As Iyov said, *"I clothed myself in righteousness and it robed me; justice was my cloak and turban" (Iyov 29:14).*

Then you will enjoy tranquility, your mind free of this world's tensions and attractions. You will rejoice in serving the Creator and delight in the secrets of wisdom you discover. You will be happy when you comprehend the truth about the lower and higher worlds, God's benevolent thoughts, His guidance and the fulfillment of His decrees in His creatures. As David said, *"The righteous shall rejoice in God and take refuge in Him" (Tehillim 64:11),* and, *"May the heart of those who seek God be glad" (ibid. 105:3);* and, *"Thus says God, 'Let not the wise man glory in his wisdom; let not the strong man glory in his strength; let not the rich man glory in his riches. For only with this may one glorify himself—contemplating and knowing Me" (Yirmeyah 9:22).*

This is the highest level of knowing God. Those who truly know

Him, cling to His service with their heart and inner being. They will fulfill the duties of the heart and the duties of the limbs with diligence and devotion, without strain and struggle, as David said, *"I have hurried and not delayed to keep Your commandments" (119:60)*, and the wise Shlomoh said, *"Happy is the man who finds wisdom" (Mishlei 3:13)*, and, *"Happy are those who act justly, who do right at all times" (Tehillim 106:3)*.

May God in His compassion place us in the midst of the *tzaddikim*, [who have reached this level] and help us to be included in their assemblies. Amen.

DUTIES OF THE HEART
GATE TEN

———◦◉◦———

The Gate of Love of God
On the Complete
Love of God

INTRODUCTION

[T he Gate of Love of God follows the Gate of Abstinence be-cause] the purpose of abstinence [from worldly delights] is to en-able you to concentrate fully on loving God, and on longing to do His bidding. Love of God is the greatest quality and the highest level of serving God a person can attain.

Everything mentioned in this book about Duties of the heart, good character traits, and devotion to God, are only rungs on the ladder leading to the lofty level we intend to explain in this Gate. The obligations and good qualities required of us—whether based on reason, Scripture, or Oral Law—are steps that lead to the ulti-mate goal of loving God. There is no higher level, nothing can sur-pass it.

Moshe linked the love of God with the acceptance of God's Oneness when he said, "*Hear, O Israel: Hashem is our God, Hashem is One,*" and continued, "*Love Hashem your God*" (*Devarim* 6:4,5). Moshe urged us repeatedly to love God, saying, ". . . *to love*

Hashem your God, to obey Him and to be close to Him" (*Devarim* 30:20). "*Being close to Him*" means loving Him faithfully and wholeheartedly, as it says, "*Sometimes a friend is closer than a brother*" (*Mishlei* 18:4).

The Torah frequently places the fear of God before the love of Him, as it says, "*And now Israel what does God want of you? Only this, that you fear Hashem your God . . . and love Him*" (*Devarim* 10:12) and "*You shall fear Hashem your God . . . and be close to Him*" (*Devarim,* 10:20). Fear of God is placed before the love of Him, because fear of God and abstinence are steps that ultimately lead to the love of God. It is impossible to love God without revering and fearing Him first. We placed the Gate of Abstinence before this Gate, because we cannot be filled with love of God as long as love of this world dwells in our hearts. Once you empty your heart of love of the mundane world, freeing it from cravings, love of God will anchor itself in your heart and establish itself in your soul to the degree that you want it and are aware of it, as it says, "*For Your just ways, O God, we look to You; we long for the Name by which You are called*" (*Yeshayah* 26:8).

We will discuss seven points about the love of God:

ONE: The Definition of the love of God.

TWO: The many kinds of love of God.

THREE: How to come to love God.

FOUR: Is it humanly possible to love God?

FIVE: Things that stand in the way of the love of God.

SIX: How to tell if a person truly loves God.

SEVEN: The way of life of those who love God.

CHAPTER ONE

THE DEFINITION OF LOVE OF GOD

———◈———

The love of God is the soul's innate longing for God, because it wants to come close to His heavenly light. These feelings are stirred in the soul because the soul is a spiritual essence that is naturally drawn to other spiritual beings and is repelled by earthy material bodies.

The Creator attached the soul to a physical body to test whether it can control this body [and make it act in accordance with His will]. When doing so He awakened in the soul the desire to attend to the body's requirements and to provide its needs. He achieved this by making the soul a partner of the body from the moment of birth. Therefore when the soul senses something beneficial for its body it longs for it, hoping for a respite from the body's ailments, just like a patient longs for a good doctor and a nurse to take care of him.

But when the soul discovers something that will enhance its real spiritual essence, it directs its attention to that, and with single-minded fascination tries to attain it. This is the pinnacle of pure love.

His body is constantly making demands, and the soul cannot help but divert his attention from its own needs and pay attention to the body's needs because it cannot enjoy peace and quiet when the body is in distress. The soul is thereby prevented from engaging in the spiritual pursuits it loves, which bring it bliss.

But when the soul realizes that it is becoming too attracted to the repulsive [physical world], being drawn to its fantasies; it understands that it neglected things that could save it in both this world and the World to Come. The soul then will change course, [and instead of trying to satisfy his bodily desires,] will surrender everything to the merciful Creator, and will turn its attention to freeing itself from the trap it is caught in and from the test it is put to.

The soul will then withdraw from the world, disdaining the body and its appetites. As a result, it will see the world with open eyes rather than through a cloud of ignorance of God and His Torah. It begins to distinguish between truth and falsehood, discovering the truth about the Creator and Divine Guide.

When the soul perceives God's great power and His magnificent grandeur it prostrates itself before Him in reverence of His awesome might and majesty. It stays in that position until the Creator reassures it and eases its fear. Filled with a desire to drink from the cup of love of God, the soul retreats into solitude to be alone with Him, to love Him, trust Him and yearn for Him. It occupies itself with nothing but the service of God, and nothing but the thoughts of Him enters its mind. It does not make a move other than to please God. It does not move its tongue other than to speak of God, praise, thank and extol Him, in the fervent hope of pleasing Him. If God bestows a favor on the soul, it is grateful; if He afflicts it, it suffers patiently and only intensifies its love for Him and trust in Him.

It is said that one of the pious men would wake up in the night and say, "My God! You starved me, left me naked, abandoned me, and deserted me [to fend for myself] in the dark of night, yet even if You were to burn me alive, I would love You and delight in You all the more!" This idea is indicated in the verse, "*Were He to kill me, I would still yearn for Him*" (*Iyov* 13:15), and the verse, "*My Beloved is like a bundle of myrrh, lodged between my breasts*" (*Shir Hashirim* 1:13), which the Sages interpreted in a figurative sense: "Though He oppresses me and makes my life unbearable, He rests between my breasts [meaning: His love pierces my heart]" (Shabbos 88b). Moshe Rabbeinu said in the same vein, "*Love Hashem your God, with all your heart, with all your soul, and with all your resources*" *(Devarim 6:5)* [which our Sages interpreted even to the point of giving up your life for Him].

CHAPTER TWO

HOW MANY KINDS OF LOVE OF GOD ARE THERE?

⸻◈⸻

There are three reasons why a servant loves his master:

One: For the favors the master does for him, and for his kindness to him. Two: Because the master overlooks his transgressions, forgiving him again and again. Three: He loves his master because he recognizes his master's awe-inspiring greatness. Thus the servant serves his master out of deep respect—not for any ulterior motive or out of fear.

So too, when it comes to the love of God: You may love God because He is kind and good to you, in the hope that He will reward you by His continued kindness. Or you may love God because He conceals your sins and overlooks your transgressions, despite the severity of your rebelliousness and your disobedience of His mitzvos. Then again you may love Him for Himself, for His honor, His greatness and exaltedness, which is the purest love of God, [because you are free of any selfish motives].

Moshe Rabbeinu urged us [to love God this way] when he said, "*Love Hashem your God with all your heart, with all your soul, and with all your resources*" (*Devarim* 6:5). We should be willing to give up our honor, our life and our possessions for God's sake. [It was necessary for Moshe to specify these three elements because] people have different attitudes with respect to their personal welfare, money or honor. Some people freely offer their life and their

money but are reluctant to give up their honor. Others are willing
to give up their money and their honor—but not their life. Then
there are people who are ready to give up their life and their
honor—but not their money. [Thus Moshe mentioned all three, to
teach us that we should be ready to give up even that which is
dearest to our hearts.]

It is also possible that when Moshe said, *"with all your heart,
with all your soul, and with all your resources"* he was referring to
the different ways people express friendship toward each other, for
there are three kinds of friends. One is generous with his money
[but is not willing to physically lend a helping hand]; another is
generous with his money and willing to lend a helping hand; a
third is generous with his money, willing to lend his friend a helping hand, and is even ready to give up his honor for him. As the
wise King Shlomoh said, *"If a man offered all his wealth to entice
you away from your love, he would be utterly scorned"* (Shir Hashirim
8:7), [meaning: If someone would offer you his entire fortune to
make you stop loving your friend, you would reject him]. And as it
says of Yehonasan and David, *"For he loved him as much as he loved
himself"* (1 Shmuel 20:17), and, *"Your love was more wondrous to
me than the love of women"* (2 Shmuel 1:26).

Moshe Rabbeinu urged that your love of God should encompass
your soul, body and possessions. You should be willing to part with
all three when it comes to loving God, not holding back any of
them when it comes to fulfilling His will. As our Sages said, "'With
all your heart' means [you should love Him] with both your incli-
nations, the *yetzer tov* and the *yetzer hara*; 'with all your soul'
means, 'even if you have to give up your life;' 'and with all your resources' means, 'with all your money'" (Yoma 82a). They also said,
"Treat His will as if it were your own will, so that He will treat your
will as if it were His will. Nullify your will before His will, so that
He will nullify the will of others before your will" (Avos 2:4).

Yet another way to interpret the passage, *"with all your heart, all
your soul and all your resources"* is, that we should love God both in
secret and openly, so that it will be obvious to everyone that we sincerely love God, inwardly and outwardly, in private and in public,

with the same intensity. As David said, *"My heart and my flesh shout for joy to the living God"* (*Tehillim* 84:3). [*"My heart"* denoting inward love of God, *"my flesh"* alluding to outward love of God.]

Finally, another underlying thought of the phrase, *"with all your heart, with all your soul and all your resources"* is that your efforts toward anything other than God should be for His Name's sake; you should not relate your love of God to the love of anything else; and, you should love only something He wants you to love, so that this love becomes incorporated with your love of Him.

CHAPTER THREE

How to Come to the Love of God

———◉———

Love of God will well up in you after having met many preliminary requirements. You will not attain this level by concentrating on love of God itself.

The preliminary requirements involve two types of dedications of the heart, two types of humility, two types of soul-searching, and two types of reflection.

The two types of dedication of the heart are: Accepting God's Oneness with single-minded commitment, and dedicating your actions to His Name and serving Him for His honor's sake alone.

The two types of humility are: Humility before God, and humility before God-fearing people and His chosen ones.

The two types of soul-searching are: Searching your heart about your obligations to God in light of His continuing kindness, and searching your heart about the fact that God conceals your transgressions and is forbearing and forgiving.

The two types of reflection are: Contemplating events of the past by studying the books of the prophets and the words of the early sages, as it says, "*I recalled the days of old, I pondered over all Your deeds*" (*Tehillim* 143:5), and reflecting on the world and the wonders of God's creation.

I have already explained the main idea of this to the best of my ability in this book, and what I said should suffice for one who understands and plans to save himself in this world and the World to Come.

If you have done this, and in addition, you abstain from worldly pleasures, are cognizant of God's omnipotent greatness and your insignificance, and you appreciate God's infinite goodness and kindness toward you—you will come to love God wholeheartedly with genuine purity of soul. You will long for God intensely and fervently, as described in the following verses, *"At night I yearn for You with all my being"* (*Yeshayah* 26:9) and *"My soul yearns for Your Name and Your mention" (ibid. v. 8), "My soul thirsts for You"* (*Tehillim* 63:2), and, *"My soul thirsts for God" (ibid. 42:3).*

The best way to reach this exalted level is to be greatly in awe of God, regarding His mitzvos with reverence, and bearing in mind that He oversees your hidden and open life and your inner and outer self. Consider too, that He guides you, and takes pity on you; He is aware of your concealed and revealed past, and future deeds and thoughts; He promised [to reward you for serving Him] and He draws you close to Him.

If you do so, you will turn to Him with your heart and mind with perfect faith. You will link yourself to Him with love and trust in His compassion, abundant grace and mercy. You will not relate your love of God to the love of anything else, and you will never fear anyone or anything as much as you fear Him.

You will never stop thinking about God, always being mindful of Him. He will be your companion when you are alone, and will dwell with you in the wilderness. A room full of people will seem empty to you, and an empty room will seem full; you will not be lonely when there are no people to socialize with. Instead, you will always rejoice in your God, delight in your Creator, try to please Him, and long to encounter Him. For it says, *"The righteous one will rejoice in God and take refuge in Him" (Tehillim 64:11),* as the prophet said, *"But as for me, in God I will rejoice, I will exult in the God of my salvation" (Chavakuk 3:18).* And as David said, *"God is my light and my salvation, whom shall I fear . . . " (Tehillim 27:1).*

CHAPTER FOUR

IS IT HUMANLY POSSIBLE TO LOVE GOD?

———◦◉◦———

Is loving God humanly possible? There are three kinds of love. With one kind of love, the lover finds it easy to give up his money, but not his body or soul. With the second kind, the lover would readily sacrifice a limb or money, as long as he can expect to stay alive. With the third kind of love, the lover would readily give up his money, body and soul.

Abraham displayed his love for God all three ways: he was generous with his money, body and soul. He was generous with his money by spending it on wayfarers in order to let them know that there is a Creator. The fact that Abraham said to the king of Sodom [who had told him to keep the spoils, after his victory over the four kings,] "*Not a thread nor a shoelace! I will not take anything that is yours*" (*Bereishis* 14:23) also proves that he did not care about money.

Avrohom was generous with his body when he joyfully performed the mitzvah of *bris milah* on himself and others as soon as he was commanded. He showed his willingness to sacrifice his life for the sake of God when he zealously prepared to offer Yitzchak as a sacrifice,[1] proving his pure love and the sincerity of his service

---

1. By his readiness to slaughter his only son, Abraham showed as much self-sacrifice as if he had given his own life (*Marpeh Lanefesh*).

to God. He thereby reached the highest level of loving God.

Not everyone can reach such an exalted level, because it is beyond human capacity and goes against human nature. In fact only through Divine assistance is it found in unique individuals. God helped that person overcome his innate instinct of survival as a reward for serving Him and observing His mitzvos faithfully, wholeheartedly and sincerely. This was the case with God's prophets and His chosen and cherished ones.

Not everyone is capable of loving G-d to the point of self-sacrifice, because it goes against human nature and the innate instinct of self-preservation. But most people can acquire the first two levels of love of God [that entail the sacrifice of money or something physical, like *milah*], as long as they do their best to meet the preliminary conditions mentioned earlier [in chapter three of this Gate].

[Although loving God by sacrificing your life for His sake is the highest form of love of God], the first two kinds of love are also perfect ways of loving God. Proof of this is Satan's statement to God, "*Does Iyov not have good reason to fear God? Why, it is You who have fenced him around, him and his household and all that he has. You have blessed his efforts, and his livestock have spread throughout the land. But lay Your hand on everything he has, [and see] if he does not blaspheme You to Your face!*" *(Iyov* 1:11,12). Satan meant to say: Iyov uses his love and fear of You like a merchant; trading it off for honor and wealth. [That does not prove that his love is sincere]. Take away the worldly blessings You have granted him and see if he remains loyal to You, and whether his love of You is genuine.

God replied, "*Behold, everything he has, is hereby given in your hands*" (*Iyov* 1:12). Satan then obliterated his possessions and killed his children. Nevertheless, Iyov changed neither outwardly nor inwardly in his attitude toward God, and he continued to love Him faithfully, saying, "*Naked did I come out of my mother's womb, and naked shall I return there. God has given, and God has taken away; blessed be the Name of God*" (*Iyov* 1:21).

God then said to Satan, "*Have you noticed My servant Iyov? There is no one like him on earth—a blameless and upright man who fears God and shuns evil,"* to which Satan replied, *"Skin for the sake of skin! Whatever a man has he will give up to save his skin! But lay a hand on his bones and his flesh, and he will surely blaspheme you to Your face"* (*Iyov.* 3-5). Satan meant to say that there are many people who give up their wealth, their wives and children [not out of love of God but] to save their own lives. You can only be sure they sincerely love You, when You test them with unbearable pain.

God replied, *"Behold, he is in your hands, only spare his life"* (ibid. 2:6). Thereupon Satan tried Iyov, as he said he would. But Iyov endured it all and remaining steadfast in his faith and his good thoughts about God, said to his wife [who goaded him to blaspheme God], *"You talk as any impious woman might talk! Should we accept only good from God, and not accept evil?* (Iyov 2:10).

We see that Iyov's love of God was pure because he readily accepted pain and the loss of his fortune. He did not criticize God's judgment, as he demonstrated when he said to his friends, *"Were He to kill me, I would still yearn for Him"(ibid. 13:15).* God praised Iyov for this, but He did not praise his friends when they reproached him. As it says, *"God said to Elifaz the Temanite, 'I am incensed at you and your two friends, for you have not spoken the truth about Me as did My servant Iyov'"* (Iyov 42:7).

God associated Iyov with two righteous men,—[Noach and Daniel]—and held the three of them up as an example, as He said, *"Noach, Daniel and Iyov—they by their righteousness would save their soul"* (Yechezkel 14:14). God then restored Iyov's property, as it says, *"God restored Iyov's fortunes . . . and God gave Iyov twice what he had before"* (ibid. 42:10).

These qualities were shared by all the early pious men who were tried and tested—like Daniel in the lion's den and his friends in the fiery furnace, the Ten Martyrs, and others who gave their lives *al kiddush Hashem.* This is the kind of love Moshe Rabbeinu had in mind when he urged, *"Love God with all your heart, with all your soul, and with all your resources"* (Devarim 6:5).

Even one who does mitzvos all the time and loves God because he expects reward in return, or because he fears punishment, either in this world or the World to Come, which is the level of most people who fulfill mitzvos, will be strengthened and helped by God to come to true love of Him. He will come to extol and exalt the Creator in a manner which is beyond human ability. As it says, "*I love those who love Me, and those who search for Me shall find Me*" (*Mishlei* 8:17), and "*But one who sins against Me destroys himself*" (*ibid. 8:36*).

CHAPTER FIVE

What Stands in the Way of Love of God?

————∎◉∎————

T here are many things that stand in the way of love of God. Failure to take the preliminary steps leading to the love of God is one, as I explained above. In the interest of brevity I will not repeat this. Hatred of those God loves and love of those He hates, is another obstacle. As it says, *"Should one give aid to the wicked and befriend those who hate God?"* (2 Divrei Hayamim 19:2); *"[Woe to those] who acquit the wicked"* (Yeshayah 5:23); *"Justifying an evildoer and condemning a righteous person, both are abominations of God"* (Mishlei 17:15); *"Those who forsake the Torah praise the wicked"* (ibid. 28:4), and, *"He who says to the guilty, 'You are innocent' will be cursed by people"* (ibid. 24:24).

CHAPTER SIX

HOW TO TELL IF A PERSON TRULY LOVES GOD

<hr/>

A person who truly loves God denies himself luxuries that might distract him from his service to God. The look of fear of God on a person's face is another sign of one who loves God, as it says, "... *so that the awe of Him shall be on your faces*" *(Shemos 20:17).*

There are two kinds of fear of God. One is fear of punishment; he fears God because he is afraid of the suffering God might inflict on him. If such a person were sure that he would not suffer, he would not fear God. Our Sages had such a person in mind when they said, "We should be concerned that perhaps they will come to observe the mitzvos for fear [of punishment and not for the sake of Heaven]" (Megillah 25b).

It is this primitive kind of fear of God our Sages spoke against when they said, "Don't be like servants who serve their master for the sake of receiving a reward" (Avos 1:3), and about which one of the pious men said, "I would be ashamed to serve God for reward or in order to avoid punishment, for then I would be like the bad servant who only does his duty because he expects a reward or fears punishment, but who otherwise would not do any work. I serve God because He should be served."

The second kind of fear of God stems from veneration of His glory, exaltedness and awesome power. This fear never leaves a person as long as he lives. This is the highest stage a person can attain;

it is the quality of "fear" described by our Sages. This fear is the gateway that leads to the purest and most intense yearning for God. Whoever reaches this level will neither fear nor love anyone but the Creator.

It is said that a pious man once found a God-fearing person sleeping in the wilderness and asked him, "How can you sleep in a place like this? Aren't you afraid of lions?" Replied the other person, "I would be ashamed if God saw me fear anything but Him!"

Another sign [that a person loves God] is when he does not care whether people praise or disdain him when he fulfills God's will by telling them to do good and to stay away from evil.

Another sign [that a person loves God] is when he willingly gives up his life, his body, his possessions and his children for the will of God, as it says, *"Because for your sake we are killed all the time"* *(Tehillim 44:23).*

Another sign [that a person loves God] is that he praises, thanks and exalts God all the time, as it says, *"My tongue will express Your righteousness"* *(Tehillim 35:28),* and *"My mouth was filled with Your praise"* *(ibid. 71:8).* Such a person would never utter God's Name in a frivolous oath, a false oath or in a curse.

A "frivolous oath" involves taking needless oaths, without being required by the court to swear. A "false oath" involves swearing falsely when taking an obligatory oath in a business dispute. A person should avoid completely swearing by God's Name, whether to affirm what is true or refute what is false, and surely not to affirm falsehood and to refute the truth. As it says, *"He who has clean hands and a pure heart, who has not taken a false oath by My soul or sworn deceitfully"* *(Tehillim 24:4),* *"To be in awe of this honored and awesome Name"* *(Devarim 28:58),* and *"But a sun of righteousness will shine for you who fear My name, with healing in its rays"* *(Malachi 3:20),* which our Sages say refers to those who are afraid to utter the Name of God needlessly (Nedarim 8b).

A "curse" includes an outright curse, an invective and a derogatory statement in which the Name of God is used. It is appalling how common people are prone to curse at the slightest provocation, in order to dramatize their insults.

To Say God Willing

Another sign [that a person loves God] is that he adds the stipulation, "God willing," whenever he plans something even if he plans to do it right away. By adding this phrase, he shows that he is afraid that he may die soon [and not be able to carry out his promise], or because he does not know whether God has decreed that he do it.

Bringing Others Closer to God

Another sign [of loving God] is guiding and directing others to serve God. Guide gently or harshly, depending on the time, the place and the class or status of the people you are addressing. For as the wise Shlomoh said, "*The wise man hearing them will gain more wisdom*" (Mishlei 1:5); "*To provide the simple with cleverness, the young with knowledge and foresight*" (ibid. v. 4).

Even if you reach the highest level of self-improvement, emulating the good traits of the prophets, their exemplary way of life and their efforts in the service and love of God, your merits will not reach the merits of a person who directs others in the service of God. The merits of those he has guided toward God are added to his merits, hour after hour, day after day.

This is comparable to two merchants who came to a country to do business. One was able to sell his merchandise at ten times his cost, thus the item he spent ten *zuz* on he sold for one hundred. The other only doubled his investment, but he invested five thousand *zuz*. The first merchant despite his great rate of profit, made only ninety *zuz*, while the other made five thousand *zuz* in spite of his small rate of profit.

So too, if you improve only yourself, your merit will be small. But if you improve others as well, your own merits will increase along with the merits of all those you have brought closer to God. As our Sages put it (Avos 5:18) , "Whoever influences the masses to become meritorious shall not be the cause of sin. Because Moshe was virtuous and made the masses virtuous, he is credited with the virtues of the masses, as it says, *'He carried out God's justice and His ordinances with Israel' (Devarim 33:21)*; and *'It shall go well with those who reprove; blessings of good things will light upon them' (Mishlei 24:25)*; and *'The teaching of truth was in his mouth, and injustice was not found on his lips' . . . and he turned away many from iniquity' (Malachi 2:6)*; and *'Those who teach righteousness to the multitudes [will shine] like the stars forever and ever' (Daniel 12:3)."*

That is why the Creator commanded us to admonish those who are lax [in their observance of the mitzvos], as it says, *"You must reproach your neighbor" (Vayikra 19:17)*. And our Sages said, "How far should you go in admonishing others? Rav said, 'To the point that people curse you;' Shmuel said, 'To the point that people hit you'" (Arachin 16b). And it says, *"One who reproves a person will later find favor" (Mishlei 28:23)*.

Another sign of one who loves God, is that he is happy and pleased with the good deeds he has done, because they bring him closer to God, yet he is not conceited about them; and he laments and bemoans his transgressions in a repentant mood. As David said, *"My eyes shed streams of water because they did not obey Your Torah" (Tehillim 119:136)*.

PRAYER AT NIGHT

Another sign [that a person loves God] is that he prostrates himself in prayer at night and fasts during the day, if he is able to do so. Prayer at night is more pure than daytime prayer for a number of reasons: because you are less distracted at night than in the day; because your desire for food and drink is less compelling at night than in the day; because you are not disturbed by social calls, such as friends who come to visit, or a colleague who wants to talk to you, or a creditor who comes to collect the money you owe; because at night your senses unwind from the tensions of the day, since you do not see and hear things that might upset you; because at night you can avoid hypocrisy, since there are few people around, in contrast to the daytime, when you are not likely to be alone; and finally, because at night you are better able to focus your thoughts on God and reflect on Him, as this is the time for all lovers to devote themselves to their beloved and for all soulmates to be alone, as it says, *"At night I yearn for you with all my being"* *(Yeshayah 26:9)*; *"On my bed at night I sought the one I love"* *(Shir Hashirim 3:1)*.

A great deal has been written in the Holy Books about prayer at night. To mention just a few verses: David said, *"In the night I remembered Your Name"* *(Tehillim 119:55)*, *"At midnight I arise to thank You for Your righteous ordinances"* *(ibid. v. 62)*, *"My eyes preceded the night watches, to meditate on Your word"* *(ibid. v. 148)*, *"I cried out at night before You"* *(ibid. 88:2)*, and many other passages, including, *"Arise, cry out in the night!"* *(Eichah 2:19)*.

Reciting "The Reproof" and "The Supplication"

I wrote some soul-stirring words in Hebrew, words that admonish and rebuke the soul encouraging it to pray, which I called, *"Tochachah,"* [The Reproof]. I followed with a composition praising and thanking God, asking and imploring Him for His forgiveness. I wrote in a gentle style, designed to arouse the feelings of a person who prays. I called it, *"Bakashah"* [The Supplication]. I placed both at the end of this book, for anyone who wants to pour out his heart in prayer, at night or in the day.

If you decide to use these texts, recite the *Tochachah* sitting. Precede it by reading some of your favorite psalms. Then recite the *Bakashah*, alternately standing upright and bowing low, to the end. Finally kneel and recite any plea you wish, followed by the psalm beginning with words, *"Praiseworthy are those whose ways are perfect"* *(Tehillim 119)*, as well as, *"The Songs of Ascents"* *(ibid. 120-134)*. If you prefer to say other prayers, or follow a different order, do so; I am merely suggesting the best way to do it.

When you recite these prayers, your intent should be pure, and you should concentrate on their meaning. Recite the prayers slowly. Do not say something unless you feel it in your heart, for a short prayer said with devotion is better than a lot said quickly and absent-mindedly. One of the pious men once put it, "Don't offer empty, unmindful praise—do it in a heartfelt way," and as David said, "*With all my heart I sought You, do not let me stray from Your commandments*" (Tehillim 119:10), "*I pleaded before You with all my heart*" (ibid. v. 58), "*My heart and my flesh pray fervently to the living God*" (ibid. 84:3).

And finally, yet another sign [that a person loves God] is his joy and delight in God Himself, in the knowledge of Him, in his desire to find favor with Him, in his happiness that he loves Him, and in his attachment to His Torah and his compassion to those who fear Him, as it says, "*I am a friend to all who fear You*" (ibid. 119:63); "*May all who seek You rejoice and be glad in You*" (ibid. 40:17); "*I rejoiced over the way of Your testimonies*" (ibid. 119:14); "*I have taken Your testimonies as my eternal heritage, for they are the joy of my heart*" (ibid. v. 111); "*I will rejoice in God, exult in the God that delivers me*" (Chavakuk 3:18).

CHAPTER SEVEN

THE WAY OF LIFE OF THOSE WHO LOVE GOD

———⚫———

Those who love God express their devotion in countless ways: They know [that] God [is the Source of all existence]. They recognize that He chose them [to serve Him] and that He guides and nurtures them. They recognize further, that while He gave them freedom of choice, He nevertheless controls everything that concerns spiritual or worldly matters. Those who love God have no doubts and firmly believe that all their activities and movements depend on God's decree and will. As a result, they do not look to improve their present condition, trusting instead that God will choose what is most beneficial for them.

God has charged us in the Torah to keep the mitzvos and to serve Him, and He discourages us from indulging in physical pleasure, therefore lovers of God pass up such delights. They pine for God, anxious to please him with heart and soul, and they do not hanker for worldly things with their empty allure. Rather, they hope that God will give them strength to carry out their goal of serving Him and fulfilling His mitzvos.

They praise and thank God for their achievements, and He, in turn, praises them for their efforts. When they are unable to do good, they apologize to Him resolving to do good at the earliest opportunity, fervently pleading with God to make it happen. This is their greatest desire and ultimate request of God, as David said,

"*I wish that my ways were firmly guided to keep Your statutes*" (*Tehillim 119:5*). The Creator commends them for their intention to serve Him, even if it was not brought to fruition, as He said to David, "*Because you had the intention to build a House for My Name, you did right to have that intention*" (*1 Melachim 8:18*).

They turn their back on worldly matters and bodily concerns, involving themselves in these things only out of necessity, because worldly concerns are irrelevant to them. They are interested in studying Torah and serving God in order to glorify Him, and observe His mitzvos. Their bodies are down on earth but their hearts become all spirit.

Having knowledge of God's glory in their hearts, they serve Him as if in the company of the holiest angels. Worldly desires fade from their hearts. Yearning for pleasure is eliminated and replaced with the desire to serve God and love Him. The *yetzer hara* in their hearts is smothered by the radiance of the Divine service that envelops them—just as candlelight fades before light of the sun. They are submissive before God, and confess their failings. They bow in service to Him, not caring about their own needs.

Though they may seem timid when you associate with them, when you enter into discussion with them you discover that they are wise. They know the answer to whatever you ask them, and they are forgiving when someone sins against them. Their faces beam with a radiant glow, and their minds think only of His words. Overflowing with love of God, they want none of the things others desire, nor do they enjoy conversing with others. Sickened by corruption, they walk the high road.

People are saved from calamities and rain falls, nourishing mankind and cattle, in the merit of these pious people. They reach these high levels, by depriving themselves for the short time [they are in this world], but in so doing they merit two worlds, [this world and the World to Come,] gaining a double share of good and a double advantage, as it says, "*Praiseworthy is the man who fears God . . .*" (*Tehillim 112*).

The Only All-Embracing Mitzvah

They find the number of mitzvos God gave them to be too few to repay Him for His favors, being that they took upon themselves to exert all their effort and self-restraint in order to cling to His service. There are six hundred thirteen mitzvos, of which three hundred sixty five are negative commandments, meaning things you may not do. Of the two hundred forty eight remaining positive mitzvos [i.e. things you must do], sixty-five are mitzvos that only the community as a whole is required to do, not individual persons. Then there are mitzvos that are limited by a time factor, like the mitzvos relating to Shabbos, Yom Tov, and Yom Kippur, [which can be done only on those specific days]. Some mitzvos are applicable only in Eretz Yisrael, like personal sacrifices, heave-offerings (*terumah*) and tithes (*ma'aseir*), and the offering of the Yom Tov sacrifice (*korban chagigah*). There are certain mitzvos that are dependent on specific factors, like circumcision, which does not apply to someone who does not have a son; the redemption of the firstborn male child, which is not required of someone who does not have a firstborn son; the construction of a railing around a roof, which does not apply to someone who does not own a house; honoring one's father and mother, which cannot be fulfilled by an orphan, and the like.

Furthermore, the pious men also thought that prohibitions, though most are applicable, can not be counted totally because a person fulfills them merely by refraining from acting. They considered their service to God insignificant, and their good deeds too few to satisfy their yearnings and longings to please God.

Searching among the mitzvos we do physically which everyone is required to fulfill at all times, in every place and under all circumstances, they found only the mitzvah of studying Torah and learning the mitzvos [to be all-embracing], as it says, "*These words that I am commanding you today must remain on your hearts. Teach them to your children and speak of them when you are at home, when traveling on the road, when you lie down and when you get up*"

(Devarim 6:6,7), which Moshe reiterated when he said, *"Teach your children to speak of them, when you are at home, when traveling on the road, when you lie down and when you get up" (Devarim 11:19).*

DUTIES OF THE HEART

They felt the [mitzvah of Torah study] inadequate to fulfill their duty to serve God. Therefore, they added ethical disciplines and worthy spiritual qualities to the basic mitzvos.

They learned from the prophets and the pious how to earn God's favor and acceptance [of their supplementary mitzvos]. These mitzvos are the *chovos halevavos,* duties of the heart, whose fundamentals we explained in this book. [The duties of the heart] are the shrouded wisdom that is hidden in the heart and inner being of the sages. When a sage speaks, it is with this wisdom, and everyone recognizes its truth and righteousness. Through the wisdom [of the duties of the heart] a sage attains the highest qualities and reaches the most precious levels of wholehearted service, loving God sincerely with his heart, soul, body and possessions, as Moshe commanded saying, *"Love God your Lord with all your heart, with all your soul, and with all your resources" (Devarim 6:5).* People on this level are closest to the level of the pristine prophets and the pious whom Scripture characterizes as *"Lovers of God"* and *"Lovers of His Name"* and about whom it says, *"I have what to bequeath to those who love Me, and I will fill their storehouses" (Mishlei 8:21).*

To be included in this inner circle, you must abandon luxuries and be oblivious of worldly concerns. When you care for your physical needs, do so in an unfeeling way—not with fervor and excitement, like someone who takes bitter medicine reluctantly, only swallowing the foul-tasting brew to cure himself.

Concentrating on business affairs adds nothing to your income; by the same token, neglecting your business does not reduce your earnings. Being concerned with business matters keeps you from Torah study and doing mitzvos, and so [by focusing on your commercial dealings] you will be the loser every way, [you will forfeit Torah study and mitzvos, and your hard work will not boost your income].

Embrace things that will be helpful to you, bringing you fulfillment in your Torah learning and worldly concerns. Break your bad habits, and be mindful of your ultimate destiny. Select reason as your king, humility as your commander, wisdom as your guide, and abstinence as your friend. Be careful, however, when acquiring good qualities: Don't overstep your limits, for you may come to ruin, just as too much oil in a lamp drowns the light. Increase your diligence in small doses, building up your patience gradually and growing step by step.

Examine your conscience and give an accounting of yourself all the time. Study this book, memorize its main ideas, observe its principles, and analyze its particulars constantly. You will then reach the most desired qualities and the ultimate stage in noble traits that please God. You will change for the better, and you will change others for the better.

Do not expect to reach this lofty level unless you clear your heart completely of all worldly concerns, just like a drunkard cannot be cured until he is completely sober. A pious man once said, "If we would be ashamed of the Creator, we would never think of the love of God while drunk on the love of this world."

Therefore, even when your body is not involved [in mundane concerns], work to rid your thoughts of [worldly matters], because your mind tends to dwell on material things even when you are not actually involved with them.

Demand this from yourself at all times. Keep mundane desires from your thoughts, replacing them with thoughts of your ultimate destiny and the duties of your heart. Reflect on them always, and you will please the Creator. He will shine His face on you [granting you spiritual growth], He will accept your good deeds, forgive your transgressions, and you will find favor in His eyes. As it says, *"I honor those who honor Me, but those who scorn Me shall be dishonored"* *(1 Shmuel 2:30).*

SUMMARY

Ten Hebrew verses, each of which relates one Gate and its theme in the order in which they were presented conclude my book. Memorize these ten lines so you can constantly think about the topics of my book and recall its basic themes.

When you serve God, these lines will remind you to dedicate yourself entirely to Him. When you are busy with worldly things, these lines will remind you to examine your inner self. When you are upset about worldly things, these lines will remind you to trust God. When you are involved in something that may make you haughty, these lines will remind you to be humble. When nothing is troubling you, these lines will remind you to reflect on the favor God has bestowed on you. When you are enjoying earthly delights, these lines will remind you to abstain from hedonistic pleasure. When you rebel against God, they will admonish you to repent. When you neglect your Torah study and are lax about your faith, these lines will remind you to be devoted to God's service. When you believe in the Oneness of God, they will remind you to do so wholeheartedly. When you pray, these verses will caution you to restrain your tongue, control your senses, suppress your desires, keep your limbs in check, scrutinize your thoughts, evaluate your actions, and adopt all other good practices and noble character traits.

May God in His mercy and greatness show you and me how to serve Him. Amen.

THE TEN VERSES

A BRIEF OUTLINE OF THE TEN GATES OF THIS BOOK

THE ONENESS OF GOD:
> My son, dedicate your soul to your Rock,
> When you recognize the Oneness of your Creator.

REFLECTION:
> Probe, explore and ponder His wonders,
> Bolster yourself with intellect and the creed of righteousness.

SERVICE OF GOD:
> Fear God, and always observe His testimonies and statutes;
> That your step never falter.

TRUST IN GOD:
> Let your heart be buttressed and supported, relying on
> The Rock Who will come to your aid.

DEDICATION OF PURPOSE:
> Perform His statutes with a pure heart for His sake,
> And do not ingratiate yourself with your fellowmen.

HUMILITY:
> Notice that every creature returns to dust;
> Be humble, for dust and a clod of earth will be your abode.

REPENTANCE:

Let the tongue of reason fight your foolishness,
And repent of your heart's audacity and your *yetzer hara*.

SELF-EXAMINATION:

With wisdom discover in your innermost thoughts
That God's ways are righteous and upright.

ABSTINENCE:

Banish childish and youthful folly from your heart,
And do not yearn for juvenile delights.

LOVE OF GOD:

In your love you will then see the Presence of the Living God,
As your soul will be committed to your Rock.

GLOSSARY

AVRAHAM - Abraham

BAALEI TESHUVA - Individuals who have returned to the Torah way of life

BAMIDBAR - The Book of Numbers

BERACHAH pl. *BERACHOS* - blessing

BEREISHIS - The Book of Genesis

BRIS MILAH - Covenant of circumcision

CHAVAKUK - Habakuk

CHOVOS HALEVAVOS - Duties of the Heart

DEVARIM - The Book of Deuteronomy

DIVREI HAYAMIM - The Book of Chronicles

EICHA - The Book of Lamentations

ERETZ YISRAEL - The Land of Israel

GEMARA - Talmud

HALACHAH - law

HASHEM - God

HOSHEA - The Book of Hosea

IYOV - Job

KIDDUSH HASHEM - Sanctification of the name of Hashem

KOHELES - Ecclesiastes

LULAV - palm branch take on Sukkos

MELACHIM - The Book of Kings

MEZUZAH - parchment scrolls containing the Shema that is placed on the doorpost.

MISHLEI - Proverbs

MITZVAH pl. *MITZVOS* - commandment

MOSHE RABBEINU - Moses our Teacher

NECHEMIA - Nehemia

NOACH - Noah

PINCHOS - Phineas

SHABBOS - The day of rest - Saturday

SHEMA - The declaration of God's Oneness said twice each day

SHEMONEH ESREI - The eighteen blessing prayer recited thrice
   daily

SHEMOS - The Book of Exodus

SHIR HASHIRIM - Song of Songs

SHLOMOH - Solomon

SHMUEL - The Book of Samuel

SUKKAH - hut used on Sukkos

SUKKOS - Festival of Tabernacles

TEFILLIN - phylacteries

TEHILLIM - Psalms

TZADDIK pl. *TZADDIKIM* - Righteous people

TZITZIS - fringes worn on a four cornered garment

VAYIKRA - The Book of Leviticus

YAAKOV - Jacob

YAMIM TOVIM - Holidays

YECHEZKEL - Ezekiel

YEHOSHUA - Joshua

YESHAYAH - Isaiah

YETZER HARA - Evil inclination

YETZER HATOV - Good inclination

YIRMIYAH - Jeremiah

YITZCHAK - Isaac